FACED WITH MAMETZ

Faced with Mametz

Garffild Lloyd Lewis

with
Lyn Ebenezer

First published in 2017

© Garffild Lloyd Lewis / Gwasg Carreg Gwalch

Published by Gwasg Carreg Gwalch,
12 Iard yr Orsaf, Llanrwst, Wales LL26 0EH
tel: 01492 642031
email: books@carreg-gwalch.com
website: www.carreg-gwalch.com

ISBN: 978–1-84524-269-5

Cover design:: Eleri Owen

*Dedicated to memory of Uncle Ellis, one of
many tens of thousands who returned alive from the
Great War but having been scarred for ever.
He was able to tell his story...home from Hell*

There he was transfigured before them.

Matthew 17:2

This is the loveliest and the warmest spot in the neighbourhood, a shelter from the cold east wind. And you would know nothing of weather and storms, only the sighing of the wind among the Glasfryn woods.

Ellis Williams as a child in Trawsfynydd,
Summer 1904

This, I believe, was the most terrifying spot you could ever imagine. You could never have envisaged such a place. Thousands were dead. Some suspended from branches, others kneeling. I heard other lads moaning without much hope of any succour. An unforgettable day for many.

Ellis Williams as a soldier in Mametz Wood,
Summer 1916

Acknowledgements

Thanks to Nansi Lloyd Lewis, Dilys Thomas, Keith O'Brien, Dwyryd Williams, Huw Chiswell of Ffranc Television and the Gaiman Museum, Patagonia.

Contents

Foreword: 8

Section One of Three – Ellis' Memoirs

    1. Ellis' Memoirs (One)   12

    2. The Recruit   26

Section Two of Three – Ellis' Memoirs

    3. Ellis' Memoirs (Two)   42

    4. Mametz Wood   58

Section Three of Three – The Operation

    5. The Transfigurators   76

    6. Ellis' Memoirs (Three)   87

    7. Family Upheavals   108

    8. My Uncle Ellis   125

Afterword   139

Addendum   142

Foreword

On Trawsfynydd's war memorial, almost three dozen of the immediate area's fallen in the Great War are named. The most famous name is that of Ellis Humphrey Evans, better known by his bardic name of 'Hedd Wyn', Crowned Bard *in absentia* at the 1917 National Eisteddfod at Birkenhead. The Chair he should have occupied was draped in black on the stage. Just weeks earlier, on 31 July, he had been killed at Pilckem Ridge. His grave at Artillery Wood Military Cemetery near Boezinge in Belgium has been a place of pilgrimage ever since.

A soldier of the Great War whose name is not included on the Trawsfynydd memorial is Ellis Williams. The reason for its absence is that Ellis made it home alive. But the farmhand that returned was not the same person who had left with the 38th Infantry Division of the Welsh Fusiliers three years earlier in October 1915. After a catastrophic and traumatic facial injury, he had received remedial surgery to such an extent that even his own father failed to recognise him.

Ellis was among the first dozen to receive what is today described as plastic surgery. This took place both during and after the Great War. The surgeon who treated him in a French hospital in Boulogne, rebuilding his features, a task involving eighteen facial operations over eighteen months, was the innovative and eccentric Auguste Valadier. A dental specialist and facial surgeon, he was known to have ferried a dentist's chair with him in his Rolls Royce Silver Ghost.

Ellis was injured in the Battle of Mametz Wood around 11 July 1916, when the Battle of the Somme was at its height. In that bloody slaughter in the woods near the village of Mametz, British dead numbered over four thousand in just over a week, the great majority of them Welshmen. There were three thousand wounded, Ellis among them. He was hit by shrapnel in the cheek, slicing off his top lip and ripping his nose off completely. When he was found unconscious on the battlefield it seemed that his death would be inevitable.

However, following Valadier's surgery, Ellis was able to return home, only to be recalled almost immediately and sent to Ireland on active duty. When he died in 1967 at 71 years of age, it seemed the story of his life was to die with him. But some years later, among his belongings, a handwritten account, recorded in his own hand, was discovered among his numerous books. Chronicling his life from boyhood to marriage in 1925, central to it is the Battle of Mametz Wood.

His is a remarkable story, already portrayed in a Welsh-language documentary on S4C based on his written memoirs. Others who fought in Mametz Wood also wrote of their experiences, among them Robert Graves, Siegfried Sassoon, Wilfred Owen and David Jones. Ellis did not enjoy such education as had been offered to these literary historians, yet his account is just as gripping and graphic. Indeed, his style of writing reveals a man with a literary potential. And despite his shocking and traumatic experiences, his is a story brimming with wry humour and irony.

As well as experiencing a facial transformation, Ellis was involved in a transformation of a different kind. One of a dozen children of a quarryman and his wife, his early memories portray a carefree life in a haven of peace and harmony. Suddenly, he is thrown into a cauldron of conflict in the hell that was Mametz Wood. When he returned to his neighbourhood, he was forced to adapt to a way of life totally different from the one he had left three years previously. He remained without any trace of rancour or bitterness, despite the fact that he could have avoided the war completely if he had not been stopped from joining three of his older brothers in Patagonia. Indeed, even after staying, he could have avoided enlistment by arguing that his work on the land was essential.

This is the remarkable story of a simple country lad who entered the conflagration of the Great War voluntarily, and who overcame a serious facial injury, returning a stranger in more than one sense. If he had not chronicled this story or if it had not been discovered, nobody would be any the wiser.

Ellis Williams probably recorded his memoirs sometime during the middle of the 1960s. At the time he was recovering from a serious operation that necessitated the amputation of one of his legs, a result of injuries suffered almost fifty years earlier on the battlefield. His jottings fill 110 pages in a lined, blue-covered exercise book. His handwriting is neat and his style concise and clear.

This, therefore, is Ellis Williams' story based on his own memoirs, as well as familial, historic and literary recollections. It is a remarkable account, an exalting story about a simple man from Trawsfynydd who was literally transfigured. It has been an honour for me to have been asked to cooperate with Garffild in preparing this remarkable story of a truly remarkable man.

Lyn Ebenezer, autumn 2016

Section One of Three

Ellis' Memoirs

Ellis' Memoirs

1

The title Ellis Williams chose for his memoirs was
'*Adgofion o Ddigwyddiadau ar Daith Bywyd*' (*Memories of
Events on Life's Journey*). He opens with his childhood at
Ty'n-y-pistyll, Trawsfynydd: 'the loveliest and the warmest
spot in the neighbourhood', where the only storms were
'the sighing of the wind that blew among the Glasfryn
trees'.

He is eight years old and at home during the school
holidays, and his mother is unwell. He describes the
kindness of neighbours who call round to tend to her as
she sits by the fire, her face rather pale. He is then told that
his mother has just given birth to a child, his little sister. He
does not name this sibling but it must have been Mary.
Records show that Mary died when she was only seven
weeks old, one of four siblings to die young. In passing, he
mentions the fact that his father is partly disabled:

*The kindness of neighbours while tending to my mother was
an immeasurable help to my father. He could then go to his
work rather than missing out. Losing a day's work meant a lot
in those days with wages so paltry. A quarryman's wages*

weren't high, especially to those with large families. I just could not understand how one… could do any work at all with just one arm.

Ellis then names some of the kindly neighbours, people such as Robert Roberts (a shoemaker) and his wife Ann, Gwen Jones and her husband (a quarryman), Mrs Cadwaladr Jones, and Elen Davies. He begins to compare the old ways of good neighbourliness he experienced in his childhood to the uncaring ways of the day, which came about despite the improvement in living standards.

When we compare today's way of life among neighbours, this is the age when it is all go, with no-one going without, all living with abundance and without hardship. This is a world that has changed so much, and with that change [it] has lost both sympathy and kindness without knowing the feeling of need and sharing the load. There is no time for such sentiments. There were no nurses we could summon back then; we could only run to fetch one of these ever-willing ladies. And old Doctor Humphrey. The women were just as good midwives as could be found anywhere. I could say much more. But let's be thankful that the world has changed, and that the change has been, in many ways, for the better.

He then turns to the joy of being in the Glasfryn fields with one of the farmhands, scattering and airing the swathes of newly mown hay. This was a way of hastening the drying process. He describes the owner of the farm, Mrs Jarret, as an authoritative lady who inspired a feeling of respectful awe from both children and adults alike. He also praises her for the nature of the food served to him and the farmhand. It would be left on the kitchen table following their labour with the haymaking.

There at the back stood the wide three-legged cauldron on the middle of the table, brimming with rice porridge made through fresh milk. It was just as good as pudding. There was a jug full of buttermilk; another jug full of milk. Everyone would help themselves. On some occasions there could be as many as four of us, in addition to the farmhand. No-one needed to ask if the fare was good. The expression on our faces as we ate spoke for us. Then Mrs Jarret would inquire whether we wanted a cup of tea. Seldom did we accept as we had by then eaten two bowls-full and found it hard to breathe. Then out we would trot like horses.

We are told that at Glasfryn there were six cows, as well as a black horse that was 'a sturdy pony and a good worker'.

The horse would also carry the Sunday preacher to Cwm Prysor and then here to Eden in the afternoon. I admired that

The family in 1898: William Williams and his wife Ellen, with Willie (right) Evan Robert and Owen (centre). John Henry is in his mother's arms and Ellis in his fathers'. The girl in front is Gwen (Winifred).

pony, believing there was no better steed anywhere. I had heard that Dei Francis, the farmhand, had caused the preacher to be thrown from the trap one Sunday. Dei was driving pretty quickly that Sunday when he came to a sharp bend. He turned so suddenly that the poor preacher had no time to hold on and was hurled from the trap over the parapet and into the river. Often I tried to persuade Dei to describe to me what exactly had happened but he was reluctant to go into details. I realised later that Dei was often tormented by being reminded of this event and was reluctant to expand upon it.

We then read of the occasional helpers or ushers, who were young lads, many of them schoolchildren. They would lead the shire horses that drew the hay-loads. Ellis is unable to hide his envy and his desire to emulate youths like his brother Owen, who was employed at Gors.

Saturday arrived, the day when the ushers would come home, as was the custom among the older youths who would be employed over the harvest. They would earn between sixpence to nine pence a day as well as earning their keep, and this was a great help to their parents. Owen came home looking every inch a man. He brought with him a can-full of milk with lumps of fresh butter floating in it. I begin questioning him and telling him how many cartloads of hay were harvested daily at Glasfryn. Then, with mam listening, Owen laughs telling me that I don't know the half of it. While we had only one horse and one hay cart they had two horses and three hay carts, and he was the one who would usher the horses to the rickyard. Then he would ride them back to the field and change them around, then taking over the dray horse pulling the wagon. This would continue for two or three hours daily when the weather was dry.

Owen would describe to Ellis his life as an underling for Robert Williams, praising his employer while Ellis listened 'open mouthed and missing nothing'. This question-and-answer would continue as they lay in bed all through Sunday night. Ellis couldn't sleep from imagining being able to accompany his brother to Gors, wherever that place might be. According to Owen, it was situated around three miles up in Cwm Prysor, and he would list the names of other farmsteads that stood along the way. One morning, a long argument ensued between Ellis and his mother.

The time has arrived and Owen is ready to leave and I am crying my eyes out. He walks off and I continue crying, with mam unable to persuade me to go back inside to avoid neighbours hearing me crying... To stop my cries waking other children, mam calls Owen back.

Their mother yields and Ellis is allowed to accompany Owen, but only as far as Rhos Hafod Wen, where Gors becomes visible. He is told to come straight home once he parts with Owen.

I was on top of the world and off I went. I was eight years old and Owen was ten. As we set off I began asking Owen the whereabouts of this place and that. We reached Rhos Hafod Wen and there stood Gors, Owen pointing it out to me. I could only see a part of the roof. Then he ordered me to go home according to what mam had made me promise. If I didn't, there would be trouble.

Ellis, however, demands to go all the way with Owen. On arriving he is invited into the house by Lizzie, the daughter, who is around twenty years old with blonde hair. According to Ellis, she was on the heavy side, 'a real farm girl'. In the house he is invited to sit at the kitchen table while Lizzie prepares some 'shot' for both boys. Shot was a mixture of oatmeal and milk, a type of thin porridge or gruel. When Ellis looks at the open fire he notices a kettle suspended from the chain above it, an appliance known as a 'crane', and he is surprised to see peat rather than coal on the fire.

After breakfast he starts chatting to an old woman, Lizzie's grandmother. He explains to her his presence and she urges him to eat his fill and to linger until after teatime as there is plenty of work for him at Gors.

This pleases him and out he goes with Owen to help gather the hay on the meadow, to feed the calves with milk, and to carry peat to the house. He spends the rest of the day helping Lizzie with the churning and by washing the floor. Reading between the lines, it seems that the eight-year-old Ellis took a fancy to Lizzie. She becomes an instant heroine.

Dinnertime arrives with Ellis still hanging around. He meets with the farmer Robert Williams, who enters with Ellis' older brother William (Willie), who has been employed at Gors for a year. Willie must have been around fifteen years old at the time. With them is Dafydd Lloyd, 'a diligent and honest man' who would, during the corn harvest season, join the harvesters in the Clwyd Valley.

On the table are new potatoes and home-cured bacon. This is followed by pudding. After the meal, Ellis is invited to join the others to harvest the hay. Teatime arrives and on the table is a bowl brimming with shot. There is also oatmeal bread, a white loaf baked in the wall oven and homemade cheese, and all those around the table are invited to help themselves. They then return to the meadow. Ellis' dream is realised.

Away we went to the meadow, Willie and Owen with a horse each and me riding on the back of Willie's horse. Dafydd Lloyd went to prepare the hayshed. We then began with Willie hoisting the hay onto one of the carts and I helping Lizzie to gather the loose hay. With one cart ready, Owen led it to the rickyard and I was allowed to fetch the other horse and cart, leading it between the rows. I felt so full of myself. The whole meadow was cleared by seven o'clock. We reached home with the last load and with Robert Williams asking,

'What are we to do with this lad? He will be tired out before he reaches home tonight. Perhaps it would be better if he stayed here. William will be attending church tomorrow and will be able to inform his mother and father that Ellis can stay all week.'

Ellis is delighted. Before bedtime he enjoys a supper of rice porridge, buttermilk and fresh milk. The following morning, we find Robert Williams mowing hay while Ellis is allowed to sleep late. He later describes Robert sitting on the horse-drawn mower, lightly touching the backs of the two shire horses with a slender switch, five or six feet in length. After breakfast, Ellis is given the task of scattering hay swathes with Owen on some ley land. Unfortunately, Owen is injured at the end of the week and is sent home. Robert Williams invites Ellis to stay. He enjoys himself to such an extent that he stays on for a whole month, returning for the next two summer seasons as well.

Following his three summers at Gors, he is hired by Ellis and Dafydd Tudor, Brynmaenllwyd, two aged bachelors whose sister Katie kept house while Annie Jones, Fronwynion, worked as their maid. Ellis Williams was around eleven years old at this point.

He vividly describes himself cutting nettles for the pigs using a sickle. It is then he notices a scythe hanging in the loft and, having seen his elders performing the task, he places the blade over his shoulder and begins honing it. But at teatime, Katie notices that Ellis' coat is shredded over the shoulder. She demands for him to take it off, and then she sees that the blade has cut through the cloth, through his shirt and all the way into his flesh, leaving vivid red scars on his shoulder. He is warned never to use a scythe again until he is bigger and older.

We move ahead one year and read of Ellis' initial contact with the Army, an experience that may well have helped shape his future.

It is the last Saturday when the school breaks for the harvest and I take a stroll to the camp to see the soldiers. I walked along towards where the Depot Battery stood and further along the road to Rhiwgoch. I reached the Post Office and the Sergeants' Mess. I lingered there to watch horses, six of them and three soldiers. I realised that they were two recruits and a Sergeant who were being drilled in driving and riding. A man came out of the Post Office addressing me in Welsh and asking if I would be interested in working there over the summer. I answered him saying that I would. The Post Master then asked me to read from a newspaper and to write one paragraph. He then inquired of my age. I answered that I had just turned twelve.

Ellis refers above to Bronaber Army Camp, established at the turn of the 20th century. It is revealed that he owned 'some shape of an iron bicycle', and that he went on to spend the summer working there, delivering telegrams. It seems that he was practically adopted by the men, as he was allowed to eat with them. He was also allowed to travel in an Army lorry between the camp and home.

Then we learn that the family has moved to a larger

house, Pantycelyn. Ellis' mother is sick. He starts helping Morris Williams, Llainwen, who teaches him to tame and train shire horses. Indeed, he is in such demand that he misses a few days of school while helping Morris to plough and spread manure. He sees little harm in losing a few days.

In his memoirs, Ellis muses on how lucky children are (at the time of his writing) to have more emphasis placed on their education. In his day, children had to start working at twelve or thirteen.

We learn that towards the end of Ellis' working summer his mother died and left his father 'a widower with seven or eight children'. The family had twelve children in total, but, as already noted, four died young. Auntie Ann from Tyddyn Mawr, Llanfachreth, moved in to keep house and look after the family. Ellis notes:

> *What remains in my memory of my mother's funeral is that of Ellis Tudor, Brynmaenllwyd, arriving with the trap and the grey horse to carry us. I well remember Gwen, Mag and Owen in the front, John Henry and myself at the back. I suppose I should be thankful that my father remained a widower, giving his all to raise us. And he succeeded surprisingly well to keep us from hunger and from suffering. Our thanks to him are enormous. He remained healthy until he reached 61 years, when that old quarry illness began affecting him badly. He died at the age of 62.*

During the two months Ellis spent as a telegram boy, the local school, known as 'the National School', closed. The pupils were sent to 'the Council School', and it is there we see that Ellis is advanced in his thinking. He wishes that the Sunday schools should be united in the same way, 'ensuring that children shouldn't have to bicker on the matter of denomination'. With Ellis' schooling coming to an end, David Jones called at the house to offer him employment as a farmhand, and Ellis left the following Monday to work at Fadfilltir, Cwm Prysor.

Farming at Fadfilltir was David Jones' grandmother, Catherine (Catrin) Davies. Ellis describes her as a devout woman, faithfully attending Sunday sermons and the *Seiat*, an evening weekday religious session. He had to sit with the old lady because he was, as he confesses in his memoirs, mischievous. He also admits that learning a new verse to recite at every Sunday sermon was difficult, and goes on to describe his duties as an underling, with one event in particular being very sad:

> *Catrin Davies had a large white cat with black spots. She thought the world of that old cat... When we arrived at the house one night we smelt something pungent, as if something was frying. Catrin Davies asked, 'Tell me, what is that smell?'*
>
> *By the time she reached the fireplace the smell became particularly strong. Catrin opened the oven. And there she found the old cat burnt to a cinder. Catrin probably had closed the oven door, not realising that the cat was inside.*

He relates other stories, such as having to lead the ass in circles in order to turn the shaft that, in turn, worked the butter churn, with the poor creature having to stop regularly because it was so weak. He also describes the old custom when neighbouring farmers and servants helped each other with the ploughing and other farm duties, also sharing the use of their horses. This was known as 'exchanging work'.

Ellis left Fadfilltir and was hired at Allhallowtide, the traditional hiring time, by Morris Jones of Bronasgellygog. Morris, according to Ellis, was a crisper at the kiln in the mill belonging to Ellis Morris, Fronolau. Ellis relates an interesting story of how he got lost in the fog searching for stray sheep with Floss, the chestnut-coloured bitch.

By the time I reached Cwm Bychan I had gathered some fifteen sheep. I was spotted by Charles Jones and he came over and informed me of around five others, and he rounded them up for me. He invited me in to eat. I ate a bellyful and the lady of the house handed me a sandwich to take with me in case I felt hungry on the way. Off I went with Charles accompanying me for a while. I was about to reach the top when the fog descended, making me feel quite concerned by the time I reached the boundary bank. Because of the fog I could see virtually nothing ahead, with all around me looking totally different.

I managed to usher the sheep through the gap in the bank, replacing the stone over the hole to stop them from returning. I was utterly unable to see the sheep. They couldn't have been far from me. I couldn't see the path either. I was beginning to tire and I remembered the sandwich, and it was good to have it. I had heard that if someone lost his way and was accompanied by a dog that the creature should be berated, and more often than not it would return home. I began castigating the bitch, but it wouldn't turn for home; it merely lay down.

I couldn't go on. I felt bad. There was no option but to start off for home, to carry on but feeling all the while that I was going nowhere. Everywhere looked completely alien and I felt totally spent. Then I felt as if I could smell peat smoke. My spirits lifted and I tried to work out the direction. Before very long I succeeded. I had reached the very top, and I was above Hafoty Bach. I found my way to the house and was given a cup of tea by Ann Jones, the fog lifting by now and I went home. It was half past six and beginning to darken.

Next, we have Ellis at the Middle Fair at Bala, a hiring fair. During the day some thirty farmers approach him to offer work. He accepts the offer of John Roberts, Cynythog Ganol, Llidiardau. He is given a shilling as a pledge, a traditional form of agreement. At the fair he also meets up with his brother Willie, who worked at Tŷ Du, Y Parc, near Bala. Ellis is given the task of feeding the cattle with the help of Bob Hughes, an aged bachelor. Two byres catered for around fifteen milking cows and a similar number of calves. There were also some thirty barren cows.

Ellis as a young man before the war

He soon discovers that a different dialect exists in the Bala area, when he is sent to one of the cowsheds to fetch something called a '*cunnog*'. He has no idea what the word means, and there is great mirth when he is told it refers to a milking vessel.

Bob Hughes was his sleeping partner, an entertaining sort of fellow who worked on the land digging trenches. Ellis experienced a difference between the customs at Bala and those at Trawsfynydd. He was not used to trenching nor hedging back home, nor to seeing moorland hay, only meadow hay. He seems to have been content with the work, however, and provides us a vivid description of the cattle:

When there was morning hoarfrost they would lie in the open, their backs white, then leaping and throwing their hooves… I was delighted to see them enjoying themselves and also believed that I was doing well as a feeder.

He then describes a most unusual sight.

One thing astonished me greatly. I was filling in a trench with Bob Hughes on the boundary with Cynythog Bella when I heard the sound of a man talking. We looked over the hedge. Who was there but Bob Davies. He was ploughing with the finest pair of shire horses I believe I had ever seen, a black horse and a dark red horse of around seven or eight years old. It was an amazing sight, the pair moving at the same pace, never stopping even on the headland and no use of the reins at all, only Bob's voice cajoling them.

Ellis began attending the small chapel at Llidiardau, where John Roberts was deacon and played the organ occasionally. Also on the organ was a young lad, John Jones. After the war, Jones would go to the Trawsfynydd area to start farming. According to Ellis, he eventually became precentor and organist at the chapel in Cwm Prysor.

Ellis often visited Y Parc, where Lizzie Roberts would wash his clothes, and he was also able to meet up with his brother Willie there. In total, he spent some eighteen months in the Bala area, sometimes travelling beyond the town to Gelligreen, Rhosygwalia.

The aforementioned John Jones had three sons: Gruffydd, Bob and Johnny. And he was also a fine tenor, a member of the Llanfor Choir. Ellis would spend time ferreting with the brothers on various Thursdays:

The brothers would thus earn some pocket money. They bred two or three ferrets. But one of them had to be muzzled or it

*would, having caught a rabbit, suck its blood and then sleep
all day. We would probably find it the following day. We
would catch a sack-full of rabbits*

Some rabbits were sold to Williams 'the Fish' at Bala,
while others were sent to Corwen by train. Eventually, Ellis
returned to Trawsfynydd and was employed, in turn, at
Fronasgellog, Bryncelynog, Llwyncrwn and Tyddyn
Garreg. On 10 July 1915, he abruptly announced that he
had joined the Army, his first step on a journey that was to
lead him all the way to hell and back.

The Recruit

At the beginning of 1914 the British Army was 710,000 strong, including 250,000 reservists. Around eighty thousand were regular soldiers who had been prepared for battle, but only some nine hundred were trained officers. By the end of the Great War, a quarter of the male population of the United Kingdom and Ireland had either joined up voluntarily or been conscripted. This totalled more than five million men: 2,670,000 of them volunteers, and 2,770,000 conscripts.

When Britain declared war against Germany in August 1914, there was an immediate call for one hundred thousand men. Early propaganda campaigns, which included the famous poster featuring Herbert Kitchener, the then Secretary of State for War, had an immediate impact.

The British press, aided by the historians of the day, played its part. Reports of German barbarism were rife; examples were given of the 'Big Bully' out to terrorise 'Brave Little Belgium'; patriotic songs were sung, stirring anthems such as 'Keep the Home Fires Burning' and uplifting marching songs such as 'It's a Long Way to Tipperary' and 'Pack Up Your Troubles in Your Old Kit Bag'. Among the chief inciters was Arthur Conan Doyle. Poets such as Rudyard Kipling wrote of the need for bravery when facing up to the enemy in the fight to defend civilised British values.

Such was the initial rush to enlist, that there became a scarcity of arms. Indeed, some recruits were forced to train using wooden replica rifles. At their barracks at Winchester, members of the 38th Regiment in 1915 were forced to use broom handles. Then there came the great disillusionment, as the sobering reality of war hit home. At the Battle of Loos between 25 September and 14 October 1915, the British Army lost almost sixty thousand men. Among them was John Kipling, whose father had urged young men like him to enlist.

Following that initial surge, as a result of huge losses on the battlefield and the realisation that the war would last for far longer than predicted, the rush to enlist slowed considerably. This led to the announcement of the Military Service Act by the Prime Minister, Herbert Asquith, in January 1916, and its implementation three months later. Ireland was exempt but Irishmen who had lived or worked on the British mainland were liable to be called up. Conscription was not announced in Ireland until 1918. It caused much unrest but still led to some 49,000 Irishmen losing their life in the Great War.

The Military Service Act of 1916 made conscription compulsory to all able-bodied and unmarried men who had been aged eighteen or more on 15 August 1915, providing they would not be 41 by 2 March 1916. In addition, all men of those ages who were unmarried or widowed without dependent children were also enlisted unless subject to an exception. This was extended to include married men in May 1916, and two years later to include those under 51.

Although nobody under the age of eighteen could enlist, it is estimated that a quarter of a million youths who were under the enlisting age signed on. One reason for their success in cheating their age was the scarcity of birth certificates. It should also be noted that recruiting officers received a half crown for every new recruit they could register, so 'turning a blind eye' was profitable in such circumstances. Medical examinations were also slipshod affairs. So what if a young lad was under eighteen? If he was strong enough and seemingly fit, what was the problem?

From the outset, Kitchener had emphasised the need for a huge military force. He was among the few who visualised a long struggle. He insisted that the consequences depended on the last million men to join up. His target was the formation of seventy divisions, with 92,000 recruited monthly. By 1915, the name of every man between eighteen and 41 was recorded as set out in the National Registration Act.

It seems that Ellis Williams needed no encouragement. But to his neighbour Ellis Humphrey Evans, the farmer-poet known as Hedd Wyn, it was a different story altogether. The family who farmed the Ysgwrn were ordered to release one of two brothers for active duty; this despite the fact that farming was a vocation regarded as one of national importance and as such was a valid reason for not having to enlist. Ellis Humphrey Evans, being the elder of the two brothers, although a committed pacifist, decided that he would go rather than his brother. In March 1917, he was released temporarily to help with the ploughing back home. Later, he was allowed a second temporary release. That summer was so wet that he stayed longer than he was allowed, which made him a deserter. He was arrested in the hayfield and taken to a cell in Blaenau Ffestiniog and then sent to the front in Belgium. On the opening day of the Battle of Passchendaele, on 31 July

1917, he was killed on Pilckem Ridge. At the Birkenhead National Eisteddfod a few weeks later, it was announced that the dead soldier had won the Chair. The ceremony went ahead with the empty Chair draped in black.

Despite the fact that Hedd Wyn was – and is – a national icon, Ellis' diary contains no mention of him. Only two miles separated the homes of the young men. In such a close community, they must have been friends. According to Gerald Williams, a nephew of Hedd Wyn and keeper of the family home, there is no doubt that they knew each other well. Indeed, there is evidence that Ellis' brother Willie and Hedd Wyn were close friends. Willie was one of three brothers who had by then emigrated to Patagonia, an event that is expanded on later in this work.

Ellis Williams joined the 4th (Reserve) Battalion of the Welsh Fusiliers as Private No. 26129. As a farmhand he could have avoided conscription. But there is nothing to suggest that his decision was not wholly voluntary. It is likely that he enlisted at Blaenau Ffestiniog, although he doesn't elaborate on this in his memoirs. Neither does he offer explanation as to his decision to enlist. One cannot escape the assumption that his experiences as a postman at the Bronaber Army Camp during his childhood shaped his decision. It is obvious from his jottings that the soldiers had taken him under their wings and that he was happy there.

In order to boost recruitment, it was General Henry Rawlinson who mooted the idea of forming brigades based on local communities. Rawlinson was to play a crucial role in the Battle of the Somme as Lieutenant Colonel of the Fourth Army. His plan was based on the assumption that men were likelier to enlist if they could train and fight among friends. The idea received the blessing of Lord Derby. These new battalions would be known as the 'pals brigades'. They could be a group of friends, fellow workers, members of sports clubs or young people's organisations; indeed, they could be any group or organisations that brought people together.

The idea took root and the first crew to answer the call was a group of brokers in the City of London. Within the first week, some further 1,600 enlisted. A similar venture in Liverpool attracted 1,500. Within a few days there were enough men to form four battalions. By the end of the first month some thirty thousand men throughout the UK had enlisted. Between 14 September 1914 and 16 June 1916, no fewer than 351 pals brigades had formed, including one made up of West Ham United supporters.

Prior to the outbreak of the war, recruitment in Wales had met with a less than enthusiastic response. Historic Welsh regiments had looked towards England for their recruits. The Royal Welsh Fusiliers were often referred to as 'the Birmingham Fusiliers'. But with the outbreak of hostilities, there was an immediate surge of willing recruits, and the pals brigades became an instant attraction.

In Wales, the call to arms was augmented by Christian clerics such as Reverend John Williams, Brynsiencyn, who appealed from the pulpit for young men to answer the call. John Williams, a Calvinistic Methodist preacher, dressed in military uniform and preached of the rights of small nations. He stressed the need for all patriotic young Welshmen to do the brave thing and enlist.

Did John Williams personally appeal to Ellis? It is quite possible. He preached throughout North Wales. We have an example of his powers of persuasion in when he preached at Ebenezer Chapel at Four-Crosses in Eifionydd. Present at the service was a young man, Griffith Jones from Llŷn. Following the address, he marched up to the deacon's chancel and, despite his mother's tearful plea, enlisted. Griffith, 23 years old, was killed at Mametz Wood. His mother turned her back on the chapel and never returned. The incident is included in Geraint Jones' book, *Epil Gwiberod yr Iwnion Jac* (*The Union Jack's Viper Progeny*). Griffith Jones was Geraint Jones' uncle.

Another reason for enlisting was unemployment and low wages. According to contemporary archives, a quarryman's wage at the Oakeley Quarry at Blaenau Ffestiniog in 1875 was £6 per month. To a family of two adults and five children, a typical-sized family dependent on the father's take-home pay, the weekly household bill would be higher than his wages. Out of his wages he would also have to pay for his own tools. The life expectancy of a quarryman in 1875 was 37 years, thirty years lower than the national average.

In 1900 came the Great Strike at Penrhyn Quarry, which saw a walkout by 2,800 men. They were locked out for three years. As a result, when work resumed, the workforce lost a third of its men. Many of them emigrated to the coalfields of South Wales. The Army was therefore a welcomed escaped for some. Ellis himself referred to men from the neighbourhood choosing the Army rather than the quarry. Enlisting meant a steady wage of a shilling a day as well as clothing and adequate feeding.

Among the first band of comrades in Wales to enlist was the City Hall staff in Cardiff. They formed the 16th Battalion. The 10th and 15th were South Wales coalminers who were dubbed 'the Rhondda Pals'. The 14th was made up of members of the Swansea Cricket and Football Club.

It is said that in Briton Ferry virtually every man of eligible age joined the forces. The Tylorstown Silver Band joined en-bloc. The press played its part by encouraging competition over recruiting between communities. Soon the recruiting offices in Cardiff and Swansea were overwhelmed.

Initially the great majority of the Welsh recruits came from Glamorganshire and Monmouthshire, as did half of all of those killed. Men from the rural communities had been more reluctant to join. Evidence later revealed that the final death toll in some rural counties was proportionally higher than it had been in the industrial southern areas. Comparatively, Merionethshire and Montgomeryshire suffered twice as many killed than their counterparts in the South Wales valleys.

It is worth elaborating on the formation of the Rhondda Pals. The founder was David Watts-Morgan, a prominent Labour politician who, in a meeting at the Tabernacle Chapel in Porth, quoted Lloyd George by stating that he wished to see a 'Welsh army' in the field made up of the race that had fought the Normans, the race that had fought for Glyndŵr. He longed to see that race of people giving a good account of themselves in the coming struggle. Sharing the platform with him was Mabon, otherwise known as Rhondda MP William Abraham; William Brace, MP for Abertillery; and Rhys Williams. Watts-Morgan would become the chief recruiter in Wales, and he was later elected MP for Rhondda West.

The formation of the pals brigades signified a U-turn in recruitment. Traditionally, it had been the gentry that were the core of the professional soldiers. But now, with a dire need for men, it seemed that the pals brigades would be the future of recruiting. They were a popular means of binding together friends and comrades, co-workers and members of various organisations.

The dream of forming battalions on the basis of friendship and comradeship seemed feasible. But the downside was that a single town or community could lose the majority of its young men in one battle. That was the fate of the Accrington Pals, or the 11th (Service) Battalion of the East Lancashire Regiment. At Serre on the opening day of the Battle of the Somme, 235 of the men were killed and a further 350 injured, all within minutes.

We have already mentioned the Rhondda Pals. During the second attack at Mametz Wood, the regiment consisted of a thousand of these men. The following morning only 135 were left to answer the roll call. The rest had either been killed or injured.

A prime example of a community of recruits was the 'territorial unit' formed by Lieutenant Colonel Charles Henry Darbishire, Chairman of the Penmaenmawr Granite Company. He himself had been rejected because he was too old. He therefore called for volunteers from among the company. In all, 133 of the workmen enlisted for the 6th Battalion of the Welsh Fusiliers. They became known as 'the Quarry Boys' and were shipped to Gallipoli. During the course of one day in August 1915, they were decimated at Suvla Bay. Among the dead was Works Manager Gus Wheeler.

The pals brigades, following so many casualties in action, were dissolved. One disillusioned soldier, John Harris from the Accrington Pals, stated wryly: 'Two years in the making. Ten minutes in the destroying. That was our history.' It should be noted that another reason for dissolving the pals brigades was the success of conscription.

Lloyd George's dream was to form a Welsh army of two divisions. This would be the first step towards establishing a Welsh Corps, a powerful unit that could contribute towards reinforcing the ethos of Welsh nationhood. The goal was to attract some fifty thousand men to the ranks. Recruitment, however, was slow, and it took a year before

that goal was achieved. The 38th was formed during the
autumn of 1914, with the unit initially of nine battalions.
This was achieved with the aid of public financial
contributions. Four more battalions were added in early
1915. Then, in the spring of that year, the ideal of forming
two divisions was abandoned in favour of a single division.
It had become obvious that Wales did not have the
necessary population to form two. The honorary chaplain
of the new division was Reverend John Williams,
Brynsiencyn.

Men such as Ellis were equipped with the divisional
uniform of grey homespun cloth, with leather webbing
holding grenades, a gasmask, and a rifle and bayonet. As
noted earlier, rifles were at a premium. Those issued would
have been the standard Lee-Enfield 3.303 SMLE Mk III,
which held ten bullets. Unfortunately, it had a tendency to
choke on any dirt or mud, so that on the muddy fields of
the Somme and Flanders, it had to be continuously
cleaned. The Germans, on the other hand, were equipped
with Mauser rifles, and although designed to hold only five
bullets, they were more dependable in such muddy terrain.

Gas was the much feared danger, but surprisingly the
number of British soldiers killed by gas was comparatively
low, some 8,100 – fewer than the total killed on the Somme
during the opening day of the battle. Ellis refers only once
to the danger of gas. But its effect could last long, and Ellis
himself was to suffer its consequences.

The weapon that was to personalise the Great War was
the machinegun. And Britain's attitude to its use was rather
different to that of the enemy. The British High Command
was dubious of the ability of the early Maxim. Indeed, the
whole ethos of deploying machineguns was not deemed to
be 'cricket'.

The Germans, however, persevered and developed

their use. With a crew of four deploying each gun they had at their disposal some twelve thousand machineguns in 1914. During the campaign, that number rose to one hundred thousand while British and French deployment could be counted only in the hundreds. This meant only two machineguns per every battalion of infantry soldiers. Gradually, the Vickers and the Lewis were adopted.

The German gun was the Maschinengewehr 08, known popularly as the 'Spandau MG 08', named after the location of the factory where they were produced in eastern Berlin. These were capable of firing between 1,200 and 3,600 bullets per minute depending on the type deployed. This was double the ability of the British machinegun. They had a maximum range of six hundred metres.

One weakness of machineguns generally was that they could only be fired over short periods as they tended to overheat and choke. But this was the weapon above all others which became responsible for decimating and mutilating the men of the 38th at Mametz Wood. It was referred to among the British soldiers as 'the daisy cutter' or 'the devil's paintbrush'. These were apt descriptions. The Germans aimed low at their enemies' legs and continued firing using the same trajectory, thus ripping the fallen soldiers to ribbons.

The image that dominates our vision of the Great War is that of the trenches and of the men being ordered to go over the top. The trench nearest to the enemy positions would be the front line. Thus, it was in the most precarious position. The tactic of excavating trenches was not a new strategy. It had featured in the American Civil War (1861–65) and the Russo-Japanese War (1904–05). But such was the dependency on trenches during the Great War that by November 1914 they extended in an unbroken network over four hundred miles, from Switzerland all the way to the North Sea.

On the Somme their excavation was comparatively easy because of the chalky nature of the soil. This meant a constant danger of the sides collapsing, so they would be reinforced with wooden planks or sandbags. These reinforcements were then surrounded by barbed wire. The proximity of enemy trenches to each other could be as close as two hundred yards. The open ground between them was No-Man's Land. Those occupying the trenches were foot infantry who would spend four-day shifts underground followed by four days above ground.

The 38th Division was based on three brigades and their units. The 113th Brigade had its four battalions of the Welsh Fusiliers: the 13th, 14th, 15th and 16th. The 114th Brigade consisted of members of the Welsh Regiment: the 10th, 13th, 14th and 15th. And the 115th Brigade was made up of four infantry battalions: the 17th, 10th and 11th South Wales Borderers, as well as the 16th Welsh. Soldiers of this new division numbered 18,500.

The 38th was the Welsh Division in more than one way. A large proportion of the men were Welsh speakers. The 1911 Census reveals that 43.5 percent of the population of Wales spoke the native tongue. Indeed, in Merionethshire some 48 percent were monoglot Welsh speakers. There are no separate figures for the percentage of Welshmen within the recruitment age who could speak the language. But a comment by one officer who served with the Fusiliers makes for some interesting reading.

Llewelyn Wyn Griffith from Llandrillo-yn-Rhos was Captain with the 15th during the Battle of Mametz Wood. He later wrote of his experiences in his war memoir, *Back to Mametz*, published in 1931. An extended edition, *Back to Mametz and Beyond*, was published in 2010. According to Griffith, a majority of those serving with the Royal Welsh Fusiliers spoke Welsh and were from a similar background to his own.

In Welsh, we could all talk freely, officers and men alike and with each other without impinging in any way on matters of military protocol that seemed to belong exclusively to the world of English. This created a bond of unity, that sense of being within an enclave within a community.

This was the Regiment in which Robert Graves, Siegfried Sassoon, David Jones, Vivian Pinto and Frank Richards all served, authors of the best of the war books. But they did not speak Welsh, and so there was a world into which they could not enter. This does not detract from the value of their books, but it impoverished them at the time. The men I knew were of my own kin because we spoke the same language, the one we had inherited, not the one we used as we learned our trade of soldiering.

He continued by creating a picture of what he meant. He described a scene on a canal bank near Ypres, where exploding shells were heard as well as machinegun fire. A rocket shot high above lit up the sky, extinguishing as it landed and thus making the darkness seem even darker. The back-up crew waited for the order to move up along the communication trenches towards the front.

They start singing, in harmony, being Welsh, a fine old Welsh hymn tune in a minor key. The Brigadier General asks me, 'Why do they always sing these mournful hymns? Why can't they sing something cheerful like other battalions?' I try to explain to him that what they are singing now is what they sang as children, as I did in chapel, in the world in which they really belong. They are being themselves, not men in uniform. They are back at home with their families, in their villages. But

he does not understand. Nor can he, with his
background.

The extensive use of the Welsh language during the
soldiers' everyday routine is confirmed by Wynn Wheldon
in an article in *The Welsh Outlook* in 1919. He, father of Sir
Huw Wheldon, was an officer in the 14th (Service)
Battalion. He noted that the Welsh language could be
heard extensively in greetings, in condemnation and in
warnings – and, of course, in hymns. All this implies that
Lord Derby's vision was proved to be a success, a means of
attracting like to like in order to create a close
comradeship.

On the other end of the spectrum, however, were those
who refused to fight. It is estimated that sixteen thousand
men refused to enlist on pacifist principles. Facing such
men was a tribunal. These hearings tended to be biased
and hostile. Should the pacifist argument be rejected, as
was usually the case, the man would be placed in an
impossible situation. The only alternatives would be either
to succumb to conscription or face arrest. There was
another possibility, which was to be involved in activities
that were regarded as being of national importance, such
as working on the land. Some 4,500 conscientious
objectors became involved in such work. Yet another
alternative was to be involved with various medical
organisations who cared for the injured on the battlefield.
One such conscientious objector was Lewis Valentine. He
spent three years as a member of the Army's Royal Medical
Corps in France and Ireland. Others who were forced or
coerced into joining the Army amounted to sixteen
thousand. Ten conscientious objectors died in jail and
around seventy died after their release as a result of abuse
suffered while incarcerated.

One prominent pacifist was Arthur Horner, General Secretary of the South Wales Miners' Federation, who became President of the Miners' Union. He refused to fight on the principle of class unity. He argued that the coalmine owners and the Government, which supported them, were closer and greater enemies than the Kaiser. He fled to Ireland and joined the Irish Citizen Army. When he tried to return to visit his family, he was arrested at Holyhead and jailed for six months. He was then refused an amnesty offered towards the end of the war and sent back to jail.

The war was only four days old when the Defence of the Realm Act (DORA) was adopted. The law was designed to help prevent invasion and to keep morale at home high. The press was subject to controls on reporting troop movements, numbers or any other operational information that could be exploited by the enemy. People who breached the regulations with intent to assist the enemy could be sentenced to death. Indeed, ten were executed under the regulations. During the conflict the law was amended and extended six times.

To return to Ellis Williams, he went from Blaenau Ffestiniog to Llandudno. It is worth noting that Henry Mostyn, Commander of the 17th Welsh Fusiliers, gathered the men together sometime during 1915 on a field at Bodysgallen for a public parade. A photograph of the event still hangs at Bodysgallen Hall. It is likely that Ellis was among them. It is also possible that the event was organised as a farewell parade for the men who left Llandudno.

During their stay in North Wales; at Rhyl; and at Kinmel Park, near Abergele, the division had very few training or travelling facilities. They left for Hazeley Down the divisional centre near Winchester. Records show that there were 6,510 soldiers and 1,718 horses based there. But yet again, resources were few and far between. Their training was minimal, and only included firing two dozen rounds on the firing range. Professional soldiers would have been allowed to fire ten times that many. Three months later, at the beginning of December, they departed from Winchester for France.

The French Army was in dire need of reinforcements at Verdun. The German Fifth Army had begun their attack on 21 February. By the end of June, they had fired 116,000 gas and explosive shells, killing around 1,600, and had advanced within three miles of Verdun. Meanwhile, the Battle of the Somme had commenced on 1 July and the British had lost almost twenty thousand men, with almost 35,000 wounded by the end of that opening day.

Section Two of Three

Ellis' Memoirs

Ellis' Memoirs

2

Let us return to Ellis' jottings, and his decision to enlist in June 1915. He does not offer any explanation for his decision. But Blaenau Ffestiniog, where he was first based as a soldier, was a place he was well acquainted with. He notes that many of his fellow soldiers were from Blaenau, Penrhyndeudraeth, Porthmadog, Dolwyddelan and the surrounding areas. And we learn from him why so many of his fellow recruits were married men; the Government, he states, paid towards the upkeep of their wives and children, with the men earning more than they would in the quarry.

Many of the men who enlisted, however, were too old, something they would soon discover when it came to running around while drilling or doing physical training among youngsters such as he, who were only around eighteen years old.

But there was no way of turning back. The Government was too much in need of soldiers, and anyone would suffice as they were volunteers. Many had rued joining up. They hadn't envisaged the war would have lasted so long and in so many different places world-wide.

And so we see in Ellis the first stirrings of doubt over his decision to enlist. He tells us that from Blaenau the men would occasionally be allowed home on leave. To him, that would mean catching the morning train at eight o'clock and returning on the three o'clock afternoon train, or sometimes on the later workers' train if there were no Thursday or Friday route marches. These exercises meant marches of between 20 and 22 miles while carrying a full pack of 76 pounds and a rifle.

Ellis and Margaret before he was sent to France

Many would be limping, their feet hurting. Others would be tired, especially the elderly men. We, the youngest, would be glad to see our beds on those nights. I believe we spent some two months at Blaenau Ffestiniog before moving to Llandudno. Llandudno was a lovely town in the summer. Men of our battalion, the 17th Royal Welsh Fusiliers were billeted in various houses.

We read of his visits to the Great Orme and the lighthouse. He would be on duty pounding the beat between the lighthouse and the pier or the West Beach, two hours each way with one soldier on duty during the day and two during the night. That meant two hours on duty and four hours' rest, alternately. Their duties included keeping watch and reporting on landings by any boat of a dubious nature, as well as ensuring that nobody could take photographs.

Ellis in his uniform before embarking

One night, Ellis apprehends a young girl taking photographs near Happy Valley. He is forced to confiscate her camera and note her particulars, this causing her no little distress. Then, a fortnight following these duties, he returns to his battalion to take up more training.

At the end of the first month he experiences a strange event. The emergency siren calls the men together. Within half an hour, Llandudno is in lock-down mode and surrounded with soldiers. Nobody can enter or leave. A warning has been received of two German spies in the town. They are arrested in the early hours at the St George Hotel.

An unfortunate event occurs one Saturday night after chancing upon an acquaintance on the street in Llandudno. Ellis is tempted to go AWOL, 'Absent Without Leave':

I was tempted by an old friend, Ellis Thomas, son of Ellen and Ellis Thomas, originally from Ynys Thomas but had moved to Tŷ Llwyd Terrace. Ellis had only been married for a few weeks and he felt very homesick. He asked me on the street whether I would accompany him home. I was in two minds but kept on walking with him towards the station. He was determined to go and kept on trying to persuade me to get a ticket as the train was due. 'I'm not going,' I said. 'And by going without permission we will be placed on the Black List. And I don't want that to happen.

It happened to be a Saturday night and by promising to return on Monday he managed to persuade me. In comes the train and off we go. Having reached Blaenau Ffestiniog it was impossible to connect with the train to Trawsfynydd. The last train had left so there was no alternative but to start off on foot. And no-one offered us a lift. We arrived around one o'clock in the morning and I threw some gravel at the window of Penygarreg, where my father was asleep. He opened the window and asked who was there? I answered that it was me, and that I had come to spend the weekend there so he opened the door. He began asking me this and that and I fell asleep. We slept in the same room. Morning came and we went out for a walk after dinner. When by the church I met with PC Davies.

The policeman had received a report that Ellis was absent without permission. But should he return promptly on Monday morning, then his punishment would be lighter.

We now jump a few weeks ahead and learn that all the men were called together for a special parade. They were told of the possibility of their battalion being combined with three others to form the 38th Division of the Welsh Fusiliers. Three battalions had already been earmarked and a fourth was needed. The 17th was chosen because, according to Ellis, it was the youngest battalion. Could the aforementioned parade at Bodysgallen's field have been organised to mark this event? If so, then Lloyd George would have been present.

Soon the men were summoned to Winchester, the town that would be home to the new 38th Division. Official records of the 38th indicate that the camp stood on

Hazeley Down. This was a transit camp built in 1915 on a 105-acre site with accommodation for 6,510 soldiers and stabling for 1,718 horses. There were shooting ranges at Larkhill and Bulford on Salisbury Plain. Ellis notes:

I had been in the Army for some five months by now and this was my first sight of the land of the English. And my first sight of Salisbury Plain and the beginning of a real soldier's life. There were huts at Winchester Camp but tents on Salisbury Plain with only one blanket, and having to lie on the ground. We practiced shooting every day.

According to 38th records, the men were visited on Salisbury Plain by Queen Mary, although Ellis does not refer to this. Then, after only a fortnight's training on the shooting ranges, the men were sent back to Winchester to replace a complement of soldiers allowed home on leave before their voyage to France. Ellis was chosen as batman to the Adjutant, meaning that he acted as the personal aide to the officer ranked next to the Colonel. He should have regarded this as a feather in his cap. But he was reluctant to accept the promotion.

I did not enjoy this duty as it meant, among other duties, tidying his room, making his bed, cleaning his boots and other chores. The chores themselves were fine. I was used to such chores. It meant I was tied, but I had no need to complain about that, especially as part of Army life. What made me uneasy was his habit of leaving loose money around his quarters. I did not like this habit of his. To me, who received a shilling a day, I felt I was being tempted and I could not feel happy about it. I suspected that I was being tested.

He took his complaint directly to the Adjutant. The officer apologised and begged Ellis to forgive him for his foolishness, confessing to sometimes returning in a rather tipsy condition, then removing money from his pockets as he changed into different clothes during the day. Indeed, he went as far as to beg Ellis to rethink and to remain as his batman; and should he happen upon any loose money in future, he would be welcome to keep it. He reminded Ellis that the troops would sail for France presently and urged him to continue serving him. But Ellis was adamant. He wished to relinquish his post so that he could remain one of the lads. And that, he confesses in his memoirs, was a huge mistake. Had he remained as batman, things would have been very different.

I can state, as I often did while in France, that I would never have seen the trenches at all. I would not have been nearer to them than around a mile. But that's how it was, and when I rejoined the lads I had lost my pre-embarkation leave. I was to sail within a week and those who were on leave were

Preparing for hell. The 38th on their way to Mametz Wood.

47

recalled even though they had only just arrived home. Came the day, I bade farewell to the old country. We all gathered our packs in preparation for our train journey from Southampton

There our ship was being loaded. We were all on board by eight o'clock. It was Saturday night, the last Saturday night for many thousands. And for over three quarters of the 38th Welsh Division.

According to some records, it is possible that the ship was a paddle steamer, the SS *Margarette*. Ellis vividly describes the ship leaving port, calm and quiet initially, but then being shaken and tossed by stormy seas, the men being thrown from side to side.

I realised we were in a storm and discovered that I was not much of a sailor. Like many of the others, I began feeling so sick that I almost prayed that the old ship would go down and end it all. Everything we had eaten came back up. But through it all we managed to catch up with some sleep and when we awoke the ship had landed at Le Havre.

There was little time to look around. We began marching through a dirty-looking town, the occupants looking unkempt and poor. We reached the rest camp having marched around ten miles. The French mile was a long mile. Perhaps this was because the land was mainly so flat. What we would describe as a hillock or a hump in Wales seeming to be a mountain.

He described the camp as a collection of green and brown tents. Following a meal and a night's sleep beneath a single blanket on the brown earth, they resumed marching through various villages. Again he describes the French peasantry as unkempt, many of them pushing light trolleys. The men marched some twenty miles a day. They realised that they were nearing the Belgian border because of the change in the language they heard spoken and the difference in dress.

Ellis slowly realised the effect of the Germans' sudden attack on Belgium. Then he recalls a shattering experience. As they marched between two neighbouring farms they encountered soldiers of the Royal Artillery. A few of the men rushed over for a chat. But one of the soldiers began crying and shouting at Ellis. He describes the heartbreaking encounter.

He was Robin Alec, who had served as a farmhand at Tyddyn Bach. This was extraordinary. It was unbelievable that I should see Robin Alec, of all people, crying like that and clinging on to me, refusing to let go. He walked with us for around a mile, talking and questioning, and was reluctant to turn back. He was so delighted to see us as there were no Welshmen among his lot. We realised now that we were not far from the front.

As they neared the front, Ellis could hear the booming of the big guns in the distance. The men's destination was a small village on the Belgian border. They were warmly welcomed by its inhabitants, although they seemed very disturbed, shouting such phrases as 'British, good; Germans no good.' They begged for food, but the soldiers had barely enough for their own needs.

It was there, in the third week of December, that the advancing soldiers were granted four days of rest. Afterwards, they reached the reserve line. The big guns had started firing and spewing their empty shells again. On the Saturday before Christmas, the soldiers arrived at the deserted town of Laventie, between Bethune and Lille.

The town was in ruins and all the inhabitants had fled. A young soldier from the Welsh Guards met the men and led them towards the trenches. The men started to question among themselves what would be their fate.

I could hear the older men talking and asking how many of us would make it through? And asking what the folk back home would say should they know we were heading for the trenches? We, the young, did not consider and more than likely did not think like them. Whatever, the messenger led us to the trenches… We turned off the road and through a field with only a hedge between us and the enemy… Shortly we were out of sight in a deep trench. In about half a mile we were among the trenches, rifles firing and the occasional 'Ping!' of bullets here and there. Whatever, we had arrived and everyone taking up their position.

In the trenches, they were instructed where and when it would be safe to observe the enemy among the firing rifles and the lights of flares above No-Man's Land. Christmas 1915 was spent in the trenches, a period of nine days.

This was when Ellis realised the difference between ordinary soldiers and full-time professional soldiers, the latter described by him as 'the King's Soldiers', meaning the Guards. The big difference, he notes, was discipline. When these called out a common soldier's name, they demanded obedience.

Ellis and the rest of the men were moved on towards a maze of trenches. The men referred to this area as 'Ghiangzi', he states. It is likely that he meant Givenchy, a village fought over as early as the latter part of 1914. Snipers were rife, says Ellis, and threatened the safety of anyone who raised their head. Some hid in branches and in ruined houses. These snipers had the advantage of being equipped with 'glasses', meaning telescopic sights on their rifles. They 'destroyed many' during daylight hours.

We also had to go to No-Man's Land to lob hand grenades at the Germans, and they did likewise to us. This we referred to as 'nerve testing'. Having managed to reach the trenches, you would tremble to your boots until your whole body would shake. Then you would be handed half a mug-full of rum to settle you and warm you. It was there as well that we saw the first snow but it was unlike the snow that was seen in the old country.

Next he refers to marching through Richebourg St Vaast, a place he describes as being most dangerous. This town, according to war historians, had been flattened by shelling. Ellis was now in the front line at a place named by the men as 'Whizbang Corner' on account of the danger of rapid travelling shells, the humming noise they made as they flew and the explosions as they landed. As he crept to look for food rations with four comrades, Ellis was wounded by shrapnel from one of the exploding shells. He was not severely hurt but his injury was deemed bad enough for him to receive treatment.

While lying in the Dressing Station he chatted with another wounded soldier. Both of them longed to be home, and Ellis was tempted to fake his injury and make it look worse than it was by rubbing mud into his wound, with the hope that it would mean being sent home. But one of the attendant nurses smelt a rat and warned him that she would report him to the doctor, who, in turn, warned Ellis against doing anything similar in future that might lead to a court martial. Although Ellis doesn't say as much, he could well have been reported for dereliction of duty, leading to serious consequences.

This open confession speaks volumes of Ellis' honesty as well as his disillusionment regarding the way the war was going. But following treatment by the nurse and given the opportunity to wash and change his underclothes, he returned within a week to the front line. And then we have from him unexpected praise for the fighting quality of the foe, the Prussian Guards.

> *They were unlike the Guards of our country. [They were] large, strong men that lived up to their names very aptly. These needed no rest night or day. These could be said to be real Germans who willingly risked their lives; venturing to No-Man's Land time and again.*

Ellis was by no means alone in his admiration for the professionalism of the Prussian Guards. We have Robert Graves in his war memoirs, *Goodbye to All That*, emphasising the physical attributes of these Prussian fighting machines. But the Prussians were also aware of the Welsh presence, states Ellis, as he and his comrades fired at them, retaliating for what he described as their constant temerity. He does not expand on this accusation.

At the front, Ellis began thinking of other soldiers from his neighbourhood. He believed that he was where Owen Thomas 'Now Tom' Jones lost one eye; somewhere near where Tom Morris, Llys Awel, lost his life; somewhere near where Griffith Llywelyn Morris was sent after unsuccessfully applying to be sent to his father, who had been camp orderly and was serving.

Ellis and his comrades were sheltering in dilapidated farm buildings that included abandoned pigsties. They were being continually bombarded. There were suspicions of a spy operating and supplying enemy gunners with information. Ellis suspected the farmer's wife. He felt it odd that the farmhouse was never targeted. Indeed, one night a flashing light was seen signalling from a bedroom window towards the position of the enemy lines. Ellis believed that this signalled information was related to the presence of British soldiers. And again, he shows his distain towards the French. They were not to be trusted, wrote Ellis.

But there was little time for thought. The men returned to the trenches which twisted and turned like snakes, and they detected underground hammering noises. These betrayed the presence of sappers from both sides digging so that explosives could be placed beneath the enemy. Indeed, one night an underground explosion buried Ellis and seven of his comrades up to their necks in earth.

Spring arrived but Ellis lost a close friend, William Arthur Jones from Ffestiniog. He was hit by a stray bullet as he returned with a crew ferrying food rations to their comrades.

Bill was one of the nicest, both quiet and kind and a very religious lad. I was thankful to have known a lad like Bill as a friend. I could honestly say that he was a friend who was even closer to me than a brother. Such were my feelings towards Bill. He had worked at Breimer's shop at Blaenau Ffestiniog before joining the Army. I was never the same after losing him and I missed him greatly.

Once again he has reason to question the sincerity of the French. Billeted with his comrades on a farm, the farmer's wife caused a stir by refusing the men permission to take clean water from the pump. The men turned on her and took water and much of her belongings as well.

Eventually, the nature of the farmhand in Ellis takes over:

By now, spring was beginning to adorn the countryside. Everything looked fruitful, the land growing green. What attracted my attention was the sight of horses, greys and whites, heavy bodied horses with clean bones and very little hair on their fetlocks. I recalled the time when I worked at Bala and seeing the smartest horses that I ever saw. They would laze around in the open and then rise, leaping and kicking their hooves. It was pure joy to see them enjoy themselves in the morning mist.

Then the men encounter the enemy face to face. Ellis believed them to be Bavarians. Soldiers on either side stared at each other over the trench parapets. Some of the opposing soldiers shouted in English, 'We don't want to fight! Don't fire, and we won't fire!' And nobody fired. Then men from the Bantam Battalion arrived, short men, just over five feet in height. Usually soldiers were expected to measure over five feet and three inches, but then the 1st and 2nd Birkenheads were formed for those under the required height. They later became the 15th and 16th of the Cheshire Regiment. The Bantams distinguished themselves at the Battle of Arras in 1917. Later, two new divisions were formed, the 35th and the 40th, before they were then demolished at the Battle of Bourton. Compared to the Bantams, Ellis and his comrades seemed tall, but side by side with the Guards they seemed very small.

Then Ellis gets his first glimpse of hell:

We had travelled for a few days towards Metz, a fairly large town that the Germans had not overly destroyed. We were in and out until the end of June with quite heavy fighting throughout the month. I was outside taking a rest one night when the sudden call came, and we marched all night and for part of the day... By morning we had reached tall trees on a hill. The place was known as Mametz Wood.

Next, we have a description of an event that is wholly consistent with descriptions by others who had fought at Mametz.

> *There was a level field before it reached the wood, the Germans firing from every direction. It was a dangerous place. We were sent to No-Man's Land nightly. However, on the third night we took twenty prisoners and two officers... We were told that one officer had revealed that we could never take the wood from our side of the attack as they [the Germans] had prepared a very strong defence. Their intent was to head towards Paris.*

Ellis' description helps us to figure out when this particular incident occurred. The Battle of Mametz Wood was fought intermittently between 1 and 12 July, its height being between 7 and 11 July. The incident referred to must have therefore happened on 10 July. We learn that Ellis and the men were diverted and told to attack from a different direction. Ellis asks rhetorically, 'Why us?' This is followed by: 'I don't know.' On the following afternoon the men of the 38th were told categorically to take the wood, and to do so before morning broke. What followed therefore must have happened between late on the night of 10 July and early the following morning.

> *I can attest that the battle in Mametz Wood was the most destructive in terms of casualties, it and Verdun, during the Great War. Three quarters of our men were lost, either killed or wounded. The bombardment began around seven o'clock. It is estimated that some two hundred of the big guns were firing. They were all aiming towards the wood while we were in the trenches awaiting orders to go over the top. Around midnight a Sergeant supplied us with a tot of rum each.*

Shortly after, liquid fire was showered over the wood. The trees were alight, creating a conflagration. It became so hot that the heat was unbearable. [At] our nearest flank the fire became less intent and we intensified the shower of shells and liquid fire aimed towards the centre of the wood. Around six o'clock, around dawn, we attacked the wood. Our greatest surprise was that there was anyone at all left alive following such fire and bombardment.

... As we moved deeper into the wood, hundreds lay dead as a result of gas released among the trees around four [o'clock] in the morning. Many of the gassed Germans hung from branches. This, I believe, was the most terrifying spot you could ever imagine. You could never have envisaged such a place. Thousands were dead. Some suspended from branches, others kneeling. I heard other lads moaning without much hope of any succour. An unforgettable day for many.

Ellis continues with his recollections. A shell explodes close by, a 'coal box' shell that emitted, upon exploding, a thick blanket of black smoke. The air is full of the sounds of moaning, dying soldiers. Ellis lies among them. Upon rising, he realises that he has been wounded.

I realised that blood was pouring down my face; I attempted to bandage myself with the first aid from my pocket... Although feeling myself getting weaker through losing blood and the hurt in my head. Then I came to a full stop and I had to sit down. After a lengthy spell I tried pressing on again. But I couldn't and had to lie down. It was now almost dark when two stretcher-bearers arrived. I was carried, I don't know how far, to the First Dressing Station. It was getting darker and I could feel my face swelling. I could only see through one eye because of the swelling. Then I was lowered and placed

among others who had been wounded, some groaning,
others moaning.

A doctor arrives. Looking at the wounded soldiers, he tells
the attendants to pick out only those likely to survive.

'Take him and him and him. But leave him [Ellis] for the time
being. He might not come through it. He has lost a lot of
blood. His pulse is not too strong either.'

Ellis could not respond verbally.

I was unable to speak because my mouth was swollen so
much and full of blood. I was furious with myself. But there
was nothing I could do but wait for another opportunity [to
be moved]. Ambulances and lorries were ferrying those who
had not been badly injured. There came another opportunity,
the little doctor himself present this time. He ordered that I
should be placed in an ambulance and taken to the First
Dressing Station.
And thus I was taken away from the sound of battle.

Mametz Wood

Let us now look closer at the Battle of Mametz Wood, through the eyes of other witnesses and various war historians who went on to record their memoirs or research. The battle, from a Welsh perspective, is comparable, say some commentators, with Aberfan, Gresford and Senghenydd. Doctor Robin Barlow, of Aberystwyth University, is among them. At the Battle of Mametz Wood, he says, needless lives were lost. And those losses were on a huge scale. Thus, they all became part of the national Welsh psyche.

Despite this, when the Great War ended there was no mention of the Battle of Mametz Wood, as such, in the annals of war. It was rather included as a footnote to the Battle of Albert. The town of Albert stands some three miles from the village of Mametz. The scene of the theatre of battle can still be seen some one thousand yards to the north-east of the village.

The Battle of Mametz Wood, however, was not even deemed significant enough to be noted as a tactical event. It was only later, following literary and historical contributions by some of those who had taken part, that it became regarded as one of the fiercest and most notorious battles of the Somme Offensive.

Writers such as Robert Graves, Siegfried Sassoon and

Frank Richards, together with Welshmen David Jones and Llewelyn Wyn Griffith, and the artist Christopher Williams, and much more recently the poet Owen Shears, have ensured that the events of the Battle of Mametz Wood will never be forgotten.

Official records reveal that the 38th suffered its first fatality in France not in battle but as a result of an accident during a grenade-throwing exercise. He was Oakley Jenkins from Tonyrefail. Officers were also injured as a result of the accident. The division then proceeded to Neuve Chapelle and were part of the defensive line between Givenchy and Laventie. Then, on 11 June, they headed for the Somme.

The Battle of Mametz Wood was fought during June 1916, at the height of the Battle of the Somme. And it was at Mametz that the 38th Welsh Division, as part of the XV Corps, was first tested in the heat of battle. This battlefield in Picardy on Bazentin Ridge was a 220-acre site around a mile in length and some three quarters of a mile across at its widest point. But as both sides were on high ground separated by a dingle, it meant a climb for whichever would attempt to take the wood.

Eight brigades were involved in the attempt to take Mametz Wood. They would embark on a northerly attack. It was confidently expected that the first wave would take the wood within a few hours. But the German defenders had been well prepared and had excavated a network of deep trenches, some as deep as forty feet. And significantly a chain of strategic machinegun positions had also been prepared.

Author and poet Siegfried Sassoon was serving in the 7th Division of the Welsh Fusiliers. *In Memoirs of an Infantry Officer*, he recalls how he and his comrades moved across the exposed slope and the thick woodland, with trees 'looming on the opposite slope... a dense wood of old trees and undergrowth... a menacing wall of gloom'. Harry Fellows, in his poem on Mametz Wood, describes 'A panoply of magnificent trees / Stretching upwards to the skies'.

Men of the 38th Division, referred to as 'Lloyd George's Army' were easily recognised by their homespun grey uniforms and their red Welsh Dragon emblems. Ellis describes the march to the front as rather quiet until they reached Givenchy en route to St Pol and the Somme. There, they were subjected to a bombardment of shells for a whole week. It was estimated that some million and a half shells were fired.

The plan was to take the German front – just over ten miles across from Maricourt to Serre – and then continue towards the east and take the secondary line between Pozieres and Grandcourt and beyond. This would clear the way for the cavalry to move behind the enemy lines over open ground. Mametz Wood, therefore, stood between the 38th and their goal. This meant that the forest was of strategic importance. Senior British officers, however, confidently believed that the wood could be taken with little bother and even less time.

But news of the Somme's disastrous first day began filtering through. On that day, 1 June, almost twenty thousand British soldiers were killed and over 35,000 injured, the greatest loss in British Army history. General Haig is reputed to have described it as a good day's work, although the comment seems to be contrived. Haig showed his realistic side when he complained that the 'New Army' did not have the necessary experience, and that men had been thrown into battle prematurely by six weeks. How much difference six weeks training would have made is pure conjecture.

When the 38th reached St Pol to plug a gap in the front line to the east of Mametz Wood, they were already exhausted, many of them lame after a march that had lasted a week. The weather was atrocious, with heavy rain and strong winds. The aim was to take the wood within a matter of hours. To their left was the 16th and to their right the 13th. The Welsh were to replace the 7th. Their initial appearance on the battlefield to relieve his battalion at Quadrangle Trench was described graphically by Siegfried Sassoon in his semi-autobiographical *Memoirs of an Infantry Officer*. He described them as 'unseasoned', numbering more than double his battalion's strength of less than four hundred.

Our little trench under the trees was inundated with a jostling company of exclamatory Welshmen. Kinjack would have called them a panicky rabble. They were mostly undersized men and as I watched them arriving at the first stage of their battle experience I had a sense of their victimisation. A little platoon officer was settling his men down with a valiant show of self-assurance. For the sake of appearances, orders of some kind had to be given, though in reality there was nothing to do except sit down and hope it didn't rain. He spoke sharply to some of them, and I felt that they were like a lot of children. It was going to be a bad look-out for two such bewildered companies, huddled up in the Quadrangle, which had been over-garrisoned by our own comparatively small contingent. Visualising that small crowd of khaki figures under the twilight of the trees, I can believe that I saw then, for the first time, how blind war destroys its victims. The sun had gone down on my own reckless brandishings, and I understood the doomed conditions of these half trained civilians who had been sent up to attack the Wood. As we moved off, Barton exclaimed, 'By God, Kangar, I'm sorry for those poor devils! Dimly he pitied them, as well he might.

It should be realised that the great majority of the 38th were raw and inexperienced. They confidently believed, like others involved in the fighting as well as those back home, that it would be all over within weeks, certainly before Christmas. By that they meant Christmas 1914. But like most soldiers in Kitchener's New Army, those at Mametz were short of arms, rifles in particular. Many had not even been shown how to fire a bullet, never mind firing at the enemy. And those rifles that were available were said to be so primitive that they were more of a danger to those firing them than those facing them.

Opposing across the rise was the elite 11/Lehr Infantry Regiment, who were part of the 3rd Division and known as 'the Prussian Guards'. Accompanying them were the 311th/163rd Regiment. These were seasoned professionals bearing the latest in arms. It was the 3rd Division Lehr Guards that supplied the Kaiser's personal escorts. At Mametz they held a tract of land that could easily be defended deep in the woods. Although the XV Corps outnumbered the Prussians three-to-one, the soldiers of the 11/Lehr had been thoroughly trained, were far more experienced and had reinforced their positions in deep trenches within the forest. They also possessed the feared 'Spandau' machineguns.

Brigadier H J Evans had forewarned his fellow officers of the danger of overconfidence. Priority, he said, would have to be afforded to nullifying the danger of the machineguns. Addressing Captain Llewelyn Wyn Griffith of the 15th Headquarters, he feared his warning might lead to being sent home for daring to question senior officers' tactics. He wryly told Griffith, 'They want butchers, not Brigadiers.'

In his memoirs, *Up to Mametz*, and later updated in *Up to Mametz and Beyond*, Griffith's comments on some of his senior colleagues, calling them both cynical and withering. He describes a Brigadier called Hickie as being 'far and away the most stupid soldier I ever met.' He was, Griffith said, 'lazy, greedy, a bore in the mess.' He continues:

> The second most stupid soldier I met was Brigadier Price-Davies, who commanded 113 Brigade in which I began my career as an officer. He won the Victoria Cross and the Distinguished Service Order in South Africa as he was too dull to be frightened...

The enemy soldiers had dug in so solidly in their trenches that the British bombardment proved to be futile. The Allies' target was an area called 'Hammerhead' due to its peculiar shape. To the left lay 'Death Valley'. To the right was Flatiron Copse. The Allies crept onwards successfully until they were within two hundred yards of the enemy. Then two machineguns began firing. Those leading the attack were cut to shreds. The machineguns, augmented by dense shelling, led to widespread casualties before the attackers had even reached the perimeter of the woods. Further attacks on the following morning by the 17th Division proved to be just as futile. The initial alone attack led to the death of 131 soldiers and five officers. Those injured numbered 138. Indeed, the total losses, dead or injured during that first day, amounted to around four hundred. Captain Griffith described the scene:

Along the bare ridge rising up to Mametz Wood our men were burying into the ground with their entrenching tools, seeking whatever cover they might take... Wounded men were crawling back from the ridge; men were crawling forward with ammunition. No attack could succeed over such ground as this, swept from front and side by machineguns at short range.

A bombardment and a third attack was organised for half past four in the afternoon. Following heavy rain, the earth was a quagmire and the telephone lines were then cut. In addition, no smoke cover was organised. Captain Griffith continued:

It was nearly midnight when we heard that the last of our men had withdrawn from that ridge and valley, leaving the ground empty, save for the bodies of those who had to fall to prove to our command that machineguns can defend a bare slope.

Brigadier Evans' prophecy regarding the folly of such an attack was realised. By the end of the next day the division was back where it started but with the loss of 177 men and three officers. General Haig put the blame squarely on the shoulders of Major General Ivor Philipps. As well as criticising his tactics, Philipps was accused of a lack of initiative. Indeed, Haig, together with Lieutenant General Henry Rawlinson, visited Philipps personally at Mametz. He replaced Philipps with Major General Watts of the 7th. Watts was immediately ordered to attack in late afternoon of 10 July.

The men of the 38th, having taken the brunt of the blame for the earlier failures, felt that they were now on trial. Lieutenant Colonel Hayes, commanding officer of the Swansea Pals, addressed the officers of the battalion: 'We are going to take that wood, but we shall lose our battalion.'

It was claimed that Philipps was dismissed on military grounds, in particular his argument for throwing a whole battalion into the attack rather than a platoon made up of some three dozen men. Philipps had been MP for Southampton for eight years and was a close friend of Lloyd George. And as the 38th was closely connected with the Chancellor, it was widely regarded by the British High Command with suspicion. In fact, the division was regarded by many as a political creation. Yes, Philipps may have been comparatively inexperienced. But he could have easily avoided being at the front at all. He could have stayed at home living a comfortable and privileged life. Yet he decided to do his duty.

Before embarking on another futile attack, the 16th Fusiliers were assembled for a religious service. Hymns were sung. Welsh speakers sang in their own language the words of 'Jesus, Lover of My Soul', while those who did not speak Welsh sang 'Abide with Me'. They were addressed by Lieutenant Colonel Ronald James Walter Carden. He said,

> Men, make your peace with God. We are going to take that position, and some of us won't come back – but we are going to take it.

The Welsh lads' tendency to sing in the trenches was reflected in a poem by Robert Graves,

> Rough pit-boys from the coaly South,
> They sang, even in the cannon's mouth;
> Like Sunday's chapel, Monday's inn,
> The death-trap sounded with their din.

Carden was badly injured from the outset. He tied a handkerchief to a stick and waved it at his men so they could observe his position. He continued to lead them until he was finally felled. Once again chaos ruled. Captain Glynn Jones, whose 14th was at the rearguard, described the scene of waves upon waves of silent men slowly moving forward. He was in the third wave as the machineguns and rifles started chattering. There was a general scene of chaos that he had difficulty in recalling other than the fact he was descending the slope at a rapid rate and realising there were bullet holes in his pockets.

Other survivors are on record describing their experiences at Mametz. The ferocity of the fighting was described by Emlyn Davies, of the 17th, who had entered Mametz Wood during the afternoon:

> Gory scenes met our gaze. Mangled corpses in khaki and in field-grey; dismembered bodies, severed heads and limbs; lumps of torn flesh halfway up the tree trunks; a Welsh Fusilier reclining on a mound, a red trickle oozing from his bayoneted throat; a South Wales Borderer and a German locked in their deadliest embraces – they had simultaneously bayoneted each other. A German gunner with jaws blown off lay against his machinegun, hand still on its trigger.

As the 14th reached the edge of the woods, some forty enemy soldiers surrendered, arms held aloft. Ellis described in his memoirs a similar scene. The men suspected a trap, but no, the Germans were taken prisoner. Records show that during the fighting some 352 enemy soldiers, including four officers, surrendered. A foothold was ultimately secured at the edge of the wood but not one single yard of ground was won without a massive effort.

As night fell the scattered men looked for shelter wherever they could. Many slept where they dropped from exhaustion after fifteen hours of continuous fighting. By dawn on 11 July, the 38th was totally scattered, the tired men roaming the woods, many of their battalions severely depleted. Captain Llewelyn Wyn Griffith described the situation.

> Equipment, ammunition, rolls of barbed wire, tins of food, gas helmets and rifles were lying about everywhere. There were more corpses than men, but there were worse sights than corpses. Limbs and mutilated trunks, here and there a detached head, forming splashes of red against the green leaves, and, as in advertisement of the horror of our way of life and death, and of our crucifixion of youth, one tree held in its branches a leg, with its torn flesh hanging down over a spray of leaf.

Ever after, he said, he could not encounter the smell of cut green timber without resurrecting the vision of the tree that flaunted a human limb. A message would now be on its way, he mused:

> ... to some quiet village in Wales, to a grey farmhouse on the slope of a hill running down to Cardigan Bay, or to a miner's cottage in a South Wales valley, a word of death, incapable in this late century of the Christian Era, of association with this manner of killing. That the sun could shine on this mad cruelty and on the quiet peace of an upland tarn near Snowdon, at what we call the same instant of time, threw a doubt upon all meaning in words. Death was warped from a thing of sadness into a screaming horror, not content with

stealing life from its shell, but trampling in lunatic fury upon the cabinet we call a corpse.

Among the attackers had been the 14th (Service) Battalion from Swansea, with 676 men. Within that single day around four hundred of the Swansea Pals were killed or wounded. Over five days of fighting, the forest was virtually destroyed as the bombardment resulted in firestorms. Every inch of ground was fought for, hand to hand. Robert Graves described the resulting scene of carnage:

It was full of dead Prussian Guards, big men, and dead Royal Welch Fusiliers *[at the time officially called 'Royal Welsh Fusiliers']* and South Wales Borderers, little men. Not a single tree in the wood remained unbroken.

Welshman David Jones, who took part in the battle, wrote a description of the fighting at Mametz Wood in his long poem 'In Parenthesis', published in 1937.

And here and there and huddled over, death-halsed to these, a Picton-five-feet-four paragon of the Line, from Newcastle Emlyn or Talgarth in Brycheiniog, lying disordered like discarded garments or crumpled chin to shin-bone like a Lambourne find.

We have another graphic description of the battlefield by Captain Llewelyn Wyn Griffith:

Even now, after all these years, this round ring of man-made hell bursts into my vision, elbowing into an infinity of distance the wall of my room, dwarfing into nothingness objects we call real. Blue sky above, a band of green trees, and a ploughed graveyard in which living men moved worm-like in and out of sight; three men digging a trench, thigh deep in the red soil, digging their own graves, as it chanced, for a bursting shell turned their shelter into a tomb; two signallers crouched in a large shell hole, waiting for a summons to move, but bearing in their patient and tired inactivity the look of dead men ready to rise at the trump of a Last Judgement.

Following the debacle, the Divisional Headquarters recalled the Welsh Division from the battlefield. The 38th was replaced by a joint force of various battalions, including a brigade from the 12th. These went ahead and cleared Mametz Wood by noon the following day without much ado and without having to face much opposition. No wonder, as the Prussians had decided to move out, believing that defending the woods wasn't worth the cost of losing more men. Prussian defenders had withstood a constant barrage of a million and a half shells over seven days. Yet the Welsh Division had managed to push the elite fighting force backwards a good mile.

The 38th were not given the satisfaction of being part of the unit that eventually cleared the woods. Rather than receiving praise for their tenacity, they were indeed almost vilified with accusations of cowardice, a stain that was to take years to cleanse. A century later, what is the verdict of history on the Battle of Mametz Wood? Is it regarded as a glorious success or as an abject failure? Siegfried Sassoon, having described his initial sighting of the men of the 38th, had this to say two days later:

... the Welsh Division, of which they were a unit, was involved in massacre and confusion. Our own occupation of Quadrangle Trench was only a prelude to the pandemonium which converted the green thickets of Mametz Wood to a desolation of skeleton trees and blackening bodies.

He concluded that the battle was 'a disastrous muddle with troops stampeding under machinegun fire.'

The final irony was that within weeks, German troops recaptured Mametz Wood and held it for the remainder of the war. Be that as it may, was it reason enough to brand the 38th with something akin to cowardice? What of their later contribution to ending the war in 1918?

According to official statistics, 46 officers and 556 other ranks of the 38th died at Mametz Wood, with 138 officers and 2,668 other ranks wounded, and six officers and 579 other ranks missing. During the actual five-day battle, the casualties numbered some eight thousand, around half of them from the 38th. This amounted to a third of the division.

The Welsh town that suffered the most per head of population was Ruthin, with 26 men killed. It is believed that four others died later from their injuries. Of the total, sixteen were killed within a week of each other. Three were only seventeen years old.

Behind the stark statistics were names, and behind those names were grieving families. Those families included the Tregaskis family of Penarth, who had emigrated to Canada. The two sons, Arthur and Leonard, returned in answer to the call. They both joined the 38th on the same day, and they were simultaneously promoted Lieutenant on the same day, and commissioned on the same day. One was shot in the head on the opening day of the battle. His brother went to try and give him succour. He was also shot dead and their bodies were discovered embraced in each other's arms.

Other Welsh brothers to die on the opening day were Thomas and Henry Hardwidge of the 15th, miners who helped form the Llynrhedynog 'A Company'. On 11 July, Thomas was hit by a sniper's bullet. Henry went over to tend to him, carrying a flask of water. They were then both shot dead by the same sniper. By the end of the year a third brother, Morgan, would be killed on a different battlefield. Another pair of brothers buried at Mametz are Ernest and Herbert Philby of the 1/8th. They were both killed on 21 August and were buried side by side.

To these may be added Henry and Charles Morgan, brothers who enlisted together at Cardiff and were killed next to one another. Then there was also Albert and Ernest Oliver, who were killed within three days of each other, the former on 7 July and the latter on 10 July.

Among the chaplains at Mametz Wood was one who was known as 'Padre Evans', a Welsh speaker. Among his duties was the task of burying the dead and offering a word of comfort over them. He was seen wandering aimlessly through the woods, muttering to himself as if in prayer. This time he wasn't looking for anonymous corpses. He was searching for the remains of his own son. He wasn't successful, so he continued burying the remains of other parents' sons.

'Padre Evans' was later identified as Reverend Peter Jones Roberts, a Welsh Methodist minister from Barmouth who had joined up as a chaplain aged 51, beyond the usual age limits. He had four sons, all of whom were commissioned into the Royal Welsh Fusiliers. The boy whom 'Padre Evans' was looking for was his eldest son, Glyn, who had been commissioned in 1915 and was serving in the 9th Battalion. He had been killed on 3 July and Roberts had spent a week searching for him.

Captain Llewelyn Wyn Griffith was there with his

younger brother, Watcyn, who had, a week earlier, spent his nineteenth birthday in a trench. At the height of the battle, he was shot while ferrying a message handed to him by his big brother to present to another officer. His remains were not discovered. Later, Griffith would lose his own son, John Frimston, in the Second World War.

Before facing the enemy for the very first time at Mametz Wood, H T Jenkins of the 17th placed a copy of the New Testament in the breast pocket of his tunic. He was shot dead through the book and through his heart. In his case as well, no remains were found.

Lieutenant Lionel Duncan Stanbury was shot dead on 7 July. His possessions were dispatched home to his parents. They included a pair of puttees, a carrier bag, an air pillow, one shirt, one towel and some razor blades. His parents also received compensation for their loss. From a total of £79.5s.10d, a sum of £10.4s was deducted because their son had not served between 8 and 31 July. He had good reason for not being present. He was dead. His remains were never found.

Frederick Hugh Roberts, former quarryman, had moved south from Bethesda to work as a miner. He survived the Senghenydd disaster because he happened to be absent from work on that day, nursing a hangover from the previous night's drinking. Less than a year later, he lost his life during the opening attack at Mametz Wood.

Corpses of soldiers from both sides remained unburied in the woods for days. On the night of 16 July, Robert Graves went looking for dead German soldiers' overcoats to use as blankets. He saw an amazing sight. In front of him lay two dead soldiers, one from either side, a South Wales Borderer and a soldier of the Lehr. Both had bayoneted each other at the same instant and were united in a death embrace, reiterating what Emlyn Davies had seen and described earlier. Mametz Wood was taken, said Captain Wyn Griffith, not by the living but by those who had died:

> The dead were the chosen, and fate had forgotten us in its eager clutching at the men who fell; they were the richer prize. They captured Mametz Wood, and in it they lie.

In addition to those who died, almost three thousand soldiers were injured at Mametz Wood. Among them was Ellis Williams of Trawsfynydd. Following the debacle, a year went by before the 38th were part of any substantial battle. Ellis was, at that time, still a patient at Boulogne.

Following their sojourn at Mametz Wood the 38th were moved on to Courcelles and then to Ypres. They became involved in minor skirmishes around the Yser Canal. Then, on the last day of July 1917, they proceeded to the outskirts of Langemark in eastern Belgium.

The next engagement for the 38th would be at Pilckem Ridge, the battle that heralded the Third Battle of Ypres. There, some 3,700 soldiers of the Fifth Army would die. Among them would be a member of the 15th Battalion of the Welsh Fusiliers, a close neighbour of Ellis Williams, Ellis Humphrey Evans, better known by his bardic name, Hedd Wyn.

Faced with Mametz

Section Three of Three

The Operation

The Transfigurators

It is estimated that over a million British servicemen were killed as a result of the Great War. Twice that number returned wounded. For many who were fortunate enough to return – or unfortunate enough, in some cases – the facial injuries suffered would disfigure them for life. It could also be argued that the psychological effects of what happened were worse than some of the disfigurements themselves.

Ironically, the trenches, intended as defensive fortifications, were also the cause of many facial casualties. While trenches were ideal for sheltering from bullets and shrapnel, soldiers' faces would be exposed whenever they tried to raise heir heads above the parapet to observe the enemy.

During the early months of the war, facial injuries were mostly ignored. Facial treatment would at best be superficial. Even less attention would be given to the traumatic effects of such injuries. Indeed, it was surprising that so many such sufferers even survived long enough to receive treatment. Yet surviving such visible injuries would often be more of a curse than a blessing. Innovative plastic surgery was to change all that.

The great majority of facial injuries on the battlefield were caused by shrapnel. Unlike straightforward and 'clean' injuries caused by bullets, exploding pieces of sharp metal would rip flesh from bone and flay the skin off skulls. Metal shards also tended to pick up foreign bodies such as bits of cloth and dirt that would contaminate wounds and cause infection. Developments in facial surgery and aftercare meant more casualties surviving, and such injuries became a challenge to the emerging facial surgeons.

The surgeon chosen by the British Army to oversee this new form of surgery was Harold Delf Gillies. Born in Dunedin in New Zealand, he studied medicine at Cambridge and qualified at Barts Royal Hospital. He was a very successful athlete, a rower and a golfer. At the outset of the war, he joined the Army Medical Corps.

Gillies was immediately shocked by the frequency and nature of facial injuries on the battlefield and demanded to be allowed to set up his own unit at Sidcup. It was there that Gillies pioneered a form of treatment he named 'maxillofacial surgery'. Up to this point, facial surgery had been regarded with suspicion. But thanks to Gillies, the treatment became an integral part of the healing process, physically and psychologically. However, it should be noted that antibiotic treatment was unheard of, and such innovative surgery could lead to even more danger than the trenches threatened.

It was soon realised that the resources at the unit were insufficient, and so Queen's Hospital was opened in the town in July 1917, equipped with over a thousand beds. There, treatment was developed further, with eleven thousand operations carried out on some five thousand patients, most of them suffering wounds caused by bullets. The hospital was later renamed Queen Mary Hospital and moved to Frognal House. In the meantime, Gillies continued his mission. After no little perseverance, he succeeded in persuading the medical authorities to establish a special ward at the Cambridge Military Hospital at Aldershot for the treatment of facial injuries.

Walter Yeo, a young sailor from Plymouth, is regarded as the first patient in Britain to have received facial plastic surgery. He was sent to the hospital on 6 August 1917, having been injured on board HMS *Warspite* during the Battle of Jutland in May 1916. He had suffered severe burns to his face, losing his eyelids. Gillies' extensive long-term treatment was so successful that Yeo was able to return to the Navy in July 1919. He died in December 1960, aged seventy.

Gillies' treatment involved grafting new skin on the sailor's face, a method he named 'flap surgery' or 'tubular pedicle surgery'. This involved taking healthy skin from another part of the body, rolling it and reconnecting both ends of the resulting tube of skin to the affected area.

In the meantime, when the British Expeditionary Force left for France, it included members of the Army Royal Medical Corps. Incredibly, there was not one dentist among them, despite the fact that over two thousand men had to be sent home during the Boer War because of dental problems. Additionally, some five thousand were classed as sick because of their lack of false teeth. And according to one old truism, 'an army that can't bite is an army that can't fight'.

Meanwhile, in 1915 at Wimereux near Boulogne, another surgeon had taken to treating soldiers suffering with facial injuries. Auguste Charles Valadier was a French-American specialising in oral injuries. His surgical methods were so innovative that he was not allowed to treat his patients without being closely supervised. Indeed, his methods were regarded with suspicion and Gillies was to oversee his work.

It is worth noting an interesting event connected with Valadier before he moved to Boulogne. Shortly before his acceptance by the British Expeditionary Force, he was summoned to treat a patient suffering with toothache, no less a man than General Haig himself. This happened around the time of the Battle of Aisne in September 1914, when Valadier still practised as a dentist. At the time, Valadier was at Abbeville, not far from Aisne. The incident is confirmed by William C Cruse of the United States Corps in a paper he wrote on Valadier, published in 1986.

Was Haig's influence helpful later in persuading the British Medical Corps to accept Valadier? This is feasible, as Haig, in the dentist's chair, wouldn't have been in the ideal situation to turn down a favour. It is also interesting to note that within a month of Haig being treated, a dozen dentists were dispatched to tend to British soldiers in France. By the end of 1916, they numbered 463, and by the end of the war there were as many as 849. This eventually led to the formation of the Army Dental Corps soon after the war ended. So it may be that some good came from Haig's toothache.

Although Gillies is still recognised as the main innovator in the field of plastic surgery, it can be argued that Valadier did not receive the acknowledgement he deserved. Born in Paris in 1873, the family emigrated to America three years later. Valadier studied medicine at Columbia University and qualified as a doctor out of the Philadelphia Dental College in 1901. He had his own practice based at Philadelphia and in New York.

By the beginning of the Great War, Valadier had returned to his widowed mother and opened a practice in a fashionable area of the city. But he volunteered as a doctor with the British Red Cross Society at Abbeville. There, he became aware of a medical field establishment near Boulogne and he offered his services. Towards the end of 1914, he was assigned to the British Expeditionary at Boulogne. He arrived in his Rolls Royce Silver Ghost driven by a chauffeur. He had customised his car to carry his medical equipment, including a dentist's chair. This must have been the very first motorised dental laboratory. Later, an ambulance was adapted to continue his work.

It is well worth elaborating on this remarkable car. The chassis number was 2643 and it had originally been ordered by Hugh Montgomery on 24 September 1913. Montgomery was a member of the exclusive Marlborough Club in London and must have been affluent. He lived at Warwick Square in London but his main residence was Bosworth Park, Nuneaton. He paid a deposit of £328 on the purchase, or £33,000 in today's money. On 28 October he paid the remaining £688. In today's money, the chassis alone would cost £100,000. It seems the order for the body and steering system was later changed, making it more of a limousine.

In October 1915, Valadier bought the car through Barker & Co. The original owner, Lieutenant Hugh Montgomery of the Irish Guards, had been killed while fighting in France.

Later, in 2015, the Rolls Royce Silver Ghost was sold by Bonhams at auction. On the chassis card, its purpose was described as 'used by Military on Home or Active Service. European War 1914/19'. It had changed hands twice since Valadier. At the time, its owner was Gary Denis Flather from Berkshire, a Queen's Counsel. It had been in his family for 48 years. His wife, Baroness Shreela Rai Flather, is a member of the House of Lords. The reserve price set for the car was between £600,000 and £800,000, and it was finally bought for £718,300.

At Boulogne, Valadier was adamant that facial wounds

caused by bullets and shrapnel should receive specialist treatment. This inspired him to establish the 13th Permanent Hospital in an old sugar warehouse. In 1917, the centre was renamed the '83rd Dublin Hospital' and moved over to Wimereux. Valadier personally paid for all equipment with profit from his private practice in Paris.

It was here that Valadier developed his innovative techniques. His method involved closing wounds as soon as possible, to save or retain as many teeth as possible, and to spray water under pressure onto the wounds, irrigating them as a means of avoiding gangrene. He invented his own spraying device by adapting a drum on wheels connected to a bicycle pump. His name for this mobile cleansing device was 'the Fire Engine'.

When Gillies was sent to oversee Valadier's work, he was initially rather critical. It appears that Valadier's pioneering work was accepted by him with some reserve. Gradually, he was converted. This is how he described him much later, in 1957:

In Boulogne there was a great fat man with sandy hair and a florid face, who had equipped his Rolls Royce with dental chair, drills and the necessary heavy metals. The name of this man was Charles Valadier. He toured about until he had filled with gold all the remaining teeth in British GHQ. With the generals strapped in his chair, he convinced them of the need of a plastic and jaw unit... the credit for establishing it, which so facilitated the later progress of plastic surgery, must go to the remarkable linguistic talents of the smooth and genial Sir Charles Valadier.

Gillies' suggestion that Valadier had taken advantage of some generals while they were in the dentist's chair lends some credence to the allegation that he influenced General Haig. We have another (kinder) physical description of Valadier by one of his patients. He was described as heavy-set with a kindly but florid face and a military moustache. He carried himself smartly and was always well dressed, wearing high boots and a Sam Browne belt. He had large hands and would treat wounds firmly but gently.

Valadier was also an accomplished horseman and was described by an unnamed fellow dentist as someone who, while on horseback, could roll a cigarette with one hand and hold the reins with the other.

It is not known how long Gillies stayed with Valadier

Major Auguste Charles Valadier, surgeon extraordinary

but he must have learnt a lot from the French-American. And his early cynicism seems to have been tempered to respect. Ellis Williams does not once mention Gillies, but one photograph does show Ellis in the company of a doctor who seems to be the man himself.

Valadier and Gillies were not the only innovators in this revolutionary treatment of facial wounds. At least two others should be referred to, Doctor Varaztad Kazanjian and Hippolyte Morestin. Kazanjian was an oral surgeon, the first ever to hold the title of 'Professor of Plastic Surgery', a post he held at the Harvard Medical School. Originally from Armenia, he emigrated to America in 1895. He was originally a dentist but volunteered at the beginning of the war to serve with the Harvard Medical Corps in a tented field hospital in northern France. It was there that he pioneered facial

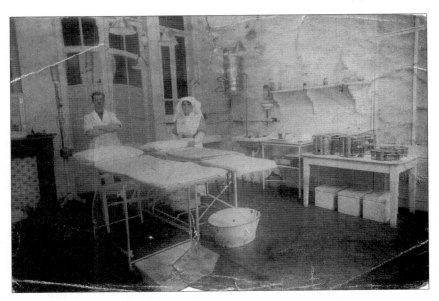

The basically equipped wards at the hospital at Boulogne

Captain Sir Harold Gillies, the pioneering facial surgeon who oversaw Valadier's early experiments

reconstruction among injured soldiers.

Morestin was a French surgeon who had studied at Paris University. As a result of his pioneering work he was dubbed 'the father of oral surgery'. He greatly influenced Gillies. They had met when Gillies worked at the British General Hospital at Rouen. Morestin was the first to successfully graft removed and rolled skin onto injured tissue, allowing new healthy skin to grow.

Facial reconstruction was still in its primitive stages at the beginning of the war. Experimentation was an integral part of the treatment and Gillies pioneered various methods he had discovered through his own research. One of his earliest successes was Lieutenant William Spreckley. Like with Ellis, the Lieutenant's nose had been destroyed. Gillies discovered during his research an old Indian method of reconstruction named 'forehead flap'. He took a section of rib cartilage and implanted it in Spreckley's forehead. There it remained for six months before being swung down and used to construct a new nose. The whole process took over three years. Spreckley was admitted to hospital in January 1917 at the age of 33 and discharged in October 1920.

Gillies pushed the limits even further. More patients survived, but the development of the various treatments still dragged. Some patients at Sidcup arrived with injuries the likes of which had never been seen before. But Gillies realised that reconstruction in itself was not enough. Attention also had to be paid to the aesthetic results. This spurred him on to more experimentation. At a time when antibiotics did not exist, it was a risky business.

He soon learnt some important lessons regarding the limits of the surgeon's scalpel. An injured pilot, Henry Lumley, arrived at the hospital, the victim of severe facial burns. Gillies took a section of skin the size of the patient's face from his chest. He grafted the piece onto Lumley's face. Soon, however, the graft became infected and Lumley died of a heart attack. From this setback, Gillies learnt that plastic reconstruction should not be performed in short stages but rather as one complete process. He realised that one end of the removed skin tissue should remain attached; then the tube formed by the rolled skin could be attached near the area where the graft would be made. This enabled him to move tissue from one location to another without the danger of infection. This 'tubed pedicle' method was a natural progression of the method used on the reconstruction of Walter Yeo's face. The live tissue was surrounded with external skin that was naturally waterproof and also prevented infection. The tube could be left in position for weeks. Gillies' method would be later developed by his cousin, Archibald McIndoe, who specialised in treating pilots with facial burns during the Second World War.

Despite these early successes, recovering patients still had to overcome psychological problems. They found it difficult to face other people and tended to try and hide their scars. Some went as far as wearing masks. Mirrors were removed from within the hospital and some patients could go for years without even glimpsing their own faces.

In the grounds and in nearby parks, benches were painted blue to denote that they were restricted to patients recovering from facial reconstruction. They would also warn the public of the possible embarrassment from encountering such sufferers. Some ex-patients found work but that work tended to be indoors and hidden away in secluded areas. Others would isolate themselves from public gaze and even from members of their own family.

As for Validier, he and his staff had, by May 1917, treated over a thousand patients suffering facial or oral disfigurements. Of these only 27 died. Among those successfully treated was Ellis Williams.

Valadier was feted and honoured. He was mentioned in dispatches three times during the war, made a Companion of Honour of St Michael and St George in 1916, and an Associate of St John of Jerusalem the following year. He was also made a Chevalier of the Legion of Honour by the French government in 1919, and in 1920 he became Knight Commander of the British Empire, in addition to receiving British citizenship.

He died of leukaemia in 1931, a pauper deep in debt as a result of gambling losses at the Le Touquet Casino. His widow received, as compensation, the derisory sum of £20 from the British Army Officers Society. But for the generosity of a rich Indian Maharaja, she would have even lost her home. What a sad end to the life of a man of vision and principle.

As for Gillies, a blue plaque adorns the wall of his old home at 71 Frognal in Hampstead, London. The actor Daniel Gillies is a descendant.

Ellis' Memoirs

3

When Ellis was ferried in an ambulance from the battlefield, his face severely disfigured, he was with two other casualties. At the First Dressing Station he was put into fresh clean clothes and relieved of his bloodied bandages. The dressings, he said, were reluctant to let go because of congealed blood. Despite his trauma at the time, he recalled being given a boiled egg to eat, as well as milk and a cup of tea to drink.

Because of his wounds Ellis could not talk, so he wrote a message asking of the extent of his injuries. The orderly replied, 'You've had it pretty bad. But cheer up, old boy; you will be in Blighty before long.'

But no, rather than being sent back to Britain, he was taken three days later to the military hospital at Boulogne. He described the journey as 'tough', with one of his fellow casualties groaning in pain. The wounded soldier was therefore left at a hospital en route and another injured soldier took his place. Upon his arrival at Boulogne, Ellis was welcomed by a nurse with a warm cup of tea. She also took his pulse.

In Boulogne he could see ships leaving port, ferrying

home injured soldiers. It must have been frustrating for him to have to stay. He was to remain there for twenty months, receiving eighteen different facial operations.

Ellis notes in his memoirs the fact that he was among the first dozen to be treated by Auguste Valadier. The facial surgeon had only been there a month. Previously, explains Ellis, Valadier had not treated humans, instead experimenting on wild animals. He then started to treat facial wounds resulting from industrial accidents.

In his memoirs, Ellis states that this Frenchman had learnt his grafting skills in America. Once war broke, he had returned to France in the hope that he could be of assistance. But, says Ellis, he was suspected of being a spy by the French government, which led the British government to step in and promote him to the honorary rank of Major, providing him with the necessary accommodation and resources to continue his specialist

A get together for the facial reconstruction patients at the Boulogne Hospital

work at Boulogne. Accommodation included an office and two wards with 32 beds. Ellis notes his views on Valadier's situation and his appearance:

He was very well to do. It was said that he was a millionaire. Judging by his attire I would not be surprised. He would buy the best clothes and boots. He was a very smart-looking man, his height around five feet ten. He would not accept wages but would do everything without any payment for the sake of the lads.

After a fortnight, the swelling in Ellis' face had receded and he could see clearly. His bed, he said, was in a desirable spot. On a clear day, he could see the White Cliffs of Dover in the distance. Within a month both wards were almost full, Ellis occupying bed six. Such was the doctor's persuasive attitude and early success, that Ellis would be given all that he asked for, including equipment and the care of numerous nurses from different countries. There were more nurses there than in the other ward, including dental nurses from Canada, Australia and from UK countries. There was also an ear, nose and throat expert: Captain Whale.

The first task involving my treatment was rebuilding my upper lip, as it had been blown away as well as all my teeth along one side and my nose. Within a month I had an upper lip and could converse. He [Valadier] had a sculptor who was able to carve a face or a skull to demonstrate what you looked like when you arrived and another to show what you would look like following the surgery. That would demonstrate what would be done and also show the difference.

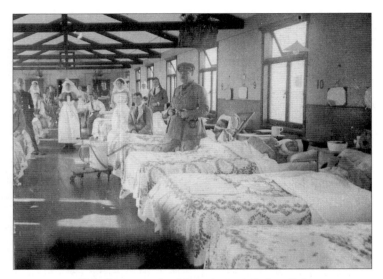

Valadier overseeing his patients at the hospital

Gillies and Valladier among the medical staff at Boulogne

These carved skull replicas were kept on shelves behind large curtains similar to those that women would draw across windows, says Ellis. He then describes the treatment in detail. The nurses would not use any ointment to lubricate the wounds but the lacerations would be washed three times a day, four if the wounds were particularly bad. He refers to Valadier's invention, 'the Fire Engine', involving the water tank on wheels and bicycle pump referred to earlier. The wounds would then be bandaged. Three nurses would be available during the day and two at night, including one Sister. Visitors would call, among them doctors and many medical students, as news of Valadier's pioneering treatment spread. He was regarded, says Ellis, as the foremost facial surgeon in France.

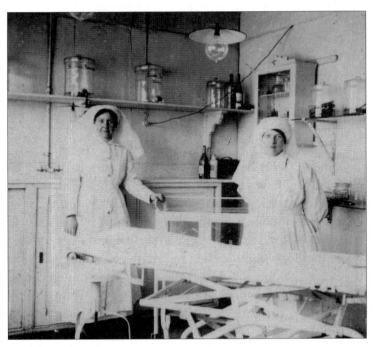

Two of the nurses preparing a bed for one of their patients

Ellis goes on to broadly explain in his memoirs Valadier's method of rebuilding a nose. He would take a section of the patient's rib and insert it beneath the flesh on the forehead. Within two months, the graft would take hold with blood flowing through the cells. Then the skin surrounding the section of rib would be cut and shaped around the cartilage. He describes the treatment that one of his fellow patients, Jock, received.

A lad from Scotland had been brought in. He had lost the whole of his jaw. Only his gullet could be seen. The doctor spent hours sitting on his bed planning how to rebuild [his jaw]. The nurse's method of feeding him was by using a beaked mug that contained some porridge or an egg mixed in milk or sometimes a drop of tea. Eventually he [Valadier] hatched a plan. Firstly, he carved the shape of the jawbone in silver and adapted it so it worked in the joint of the jaw. He then cut a piece of skin on his [the patient's] chest, turned it over and sewed and shaped it alternatively until it became the right shape. He then placed false teeth on it and when he had finished, Jock could eat everything and you couldn't say there was anything wrong with him.

Valadier went much further than his surgical duties by contributing £1 per week to Jock from his own pocket. This was to acknowledge the young Scotsman acting as the occasional model in exhibitions organised by Valadier to show how successful the surgeon's treatments were. Later, he helped Jock in securing a hundred-percent pension for the rest of his life. Previously the young man only received a fifty-percent payment of £1 a week.

Ellis then returns to describe his own treatment. Initially, it failed. Skin was taken from his left arm and replaced on his face and kept in place with plaster of Paris and kept warm with a hot water bottle. He had to lie on his bed without moving for six weeks. But when the bandages were removed, the graft hadn't taken.

This was when Valadier decided to take a section of a rib from Ellis as a foundation for his nose. Since Ellis was so strong and healthy, he was asked whether he would allow Valadier to take another piece of rib from him to reconstruct a fellow sufferer's face. Ellis agreed and both patients were treated on adjoining beds. And then we have Ellis confessing to a misdemeanour:

> I have to admit that I am one that can suddenly turn wild rather quickly. At least, I was when I was young. I was about to go under the knife one time and there were students present in the Operation Room. Usually it would be Captain Whale who would provide the chloroform. It wasn't a serious operation and I would have regained consciousness within half an hour… I realised later that one of the students had been in charge of allowing a drop occasionally to keep me asleep… I almost suffocated. I suddenly jumped up on my feet.

In other words, Ellis was awake when he should have been comatose under the effects of chloroform. So at the next operation, Ellis refused to allow the student to anaesthetise him. When he came to, he learnt he had slept for two whole nights, and he realised that it was the same student who had anaesthetised him. He relates what happened the following morning:

> I immediately became antagonised. As I was in bed No. 6 I wasn't far from the door. I grabbed a mug off the locker and threw it at him [the student]. As it happened I hit the doorframe and the mug shattered and the shards scratched

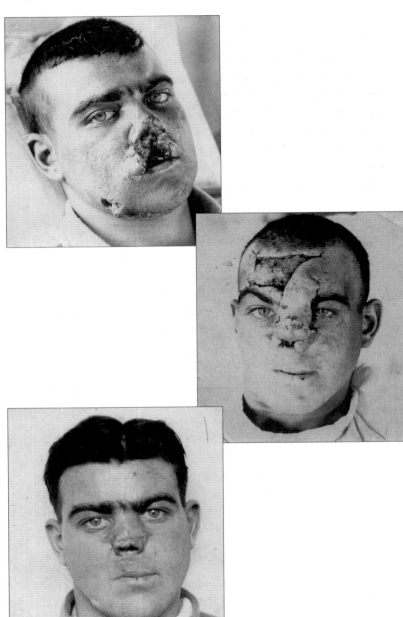

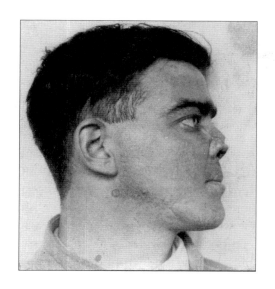

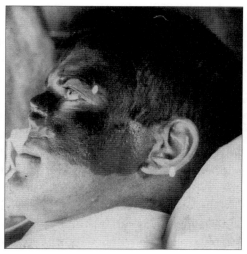

Stages in the recovery of Ellis Williams at Boulogne

his face slightly. He was soon off to the other ward. Then the doctor himself arrived and told me the student was not to blame. I answered telling him that the student should stay out of my way… I wasn't prepared to risk placing my life in his hands.

Ellis never saw the student again. Then we have another dramatic event. There was an altercation between the head nurse, who was from Northern Ireland, and a nurse from Southern Ireland. Things got heated and the two women began fighting. The bone of contention, says Ellis, was Irish politics. Both women were scratching and pulling each other's hair. They could not be separated. The head nurse received a slap, says Ellis, but the nurse from the south was never seen there again. Ellis comments on the event, understating the situation as usual:

I became aware that things were bad between the South and the North. Mentioning Sinn Féin seemed to cause some bother.

Ellis received a letter from home informing him that Robin Owen of Bromfield, Bronaber, was in a Rouen hospital. He died of his wounds the following day. Ellis suddenly realised that a girl he had seen passing through the ward was Robin's sister.

Ellis was then told that another neighbour, one he knew as 'Davies', was in a nearby hospital. He was given permission to go with a fellow patient from Canada named Oxford to borrow some khaki so that they could visit him. They encountered Davies standing on a table, entertaining the patients and staff. He was imitating Humphrey Jones, Hafoty Bach, handling a dog at the Trawsfynydd sheepdog trials. Davies was sweating profusely with the whole ward laughing. Davies, he says, was quite a card, and Ellis suspected he had deceived the authorities into believing he was sick so that he could leave his battalion, the 17th. He had done something similar in Llandudno, notes Ellis, when it was announced that the battalion was to be moved abroad.

Meanwhile, the treatment continued. Following one operation, Ellis suffering with a haemorrhage, discovered a further reason for hating the French. He, with Jock and Oxford, were strolling around the grounds when they noticed what must have been a familiar scene for Ellis, a farmer ploughing his field. His methods, however, were unlike those of a Trawsfynydd ploughman.

The farmer is on horseback, and his wife struggles between the handles of her wooden plough. He dismounts and lays himself down at the edge of the field and falls asleep while his wife continues labouring. This continues through the afternoon and evening. Eventually, the three friends decide they can stand no more of this, so they walk over to confront the farmer. He can't understand them, and Oxford grabs him by the collar and drags him to the plough. But again, neither the farmer nor his wife can comprehend. The farmer eventually threatens to report them to the hospital authorities, but nothing comes of it.

One day, all of the patients are informed of an impending visit after dinner by someone important. Those patients that are able enough are ordered to clean and tidy their ward. All patients who are fit enough are then told to stand by their beds. Two very important people then enter.

The King, together with the Queen, visited us because he had heard of the doctor's work. David Lloyd George, Prime Minister, had come over to visit the trenches. The war situation was getting better with the Germans retreating in

> *many areas. The King shook hands with all of us… The Queen held my nose and asked me whether it was attached. After they left we were entertained with a tea party and concert.*

Not everyone could claim that their nose had been grabbed by the Queen.

As is apparent, the visitors were King George V and Queen Mary, who had been told of Valadier's surgical successes. His work must have impressed the King in particular, because a few weeks later Valadier was invited over to London. He was also persuaded to take on more work, and the hospital was extended to include a ward for officers. Students from all over the world would travel to witness him at work. Ellis remembered a group of thirty, including students from China and India. Ellis and Jock were invited to open the curtains to exhibit the bust models, by then numbering around forty. So lifelike were the busts, that some of the students would faint while others needed a glass of water.

Over in England, the King was eager to see Valadier treating patients there. A suitable patient was found at St George's Hospital. His treatment had failed, so Valadier took over while other surgeons observed the treatment. But that wasn't enough. They wanted to see the whole process from beginning to end. So a suitable facially damaged patient from France was selected and the King himself observed the treatment. Valadier returned to Boulogne with a blue ribbon pinned on his chest.

When Christmas arrived in 1917, the Germans attempted to bomb the hospital. Luckily, nobody was killed. Finally, the long-awaited good news came; Ellis and his friend Jock were told they would be allowed to go home.

A postcard sent home by Ellis showing the troop carrier SS Invictia

> *The day of our leaving arrived. We left at five in the morning*
> *for the harbour and our ship. As the ship sailed out it was*
> *dawning. When we reached Southampton it was a fine day.*
> *We ended up in Whipps Cross Hospital.*

After three days there, at Waltham Forest near London, the
matron gave them permission to visit the town and to
travel on the buses without having to pay. Here, we have
confirmation of the fact that they were to don special
clothing to distinguish them from ordinary members of
the public:

> *Jock and I would get ready every day in time to catch the one*
> *o'clock bus. Very few patients in the hospital could stand as*
> *they were all suffering. Because we wore the blue suit and red*
> *tie, everyone was very kind, some even taking us to tea and to*
> *the pictures.*

Because of the shortage of beds and the fact that Ellis and Jock were comparatively healthy, they were transferred to Romford Union Hospital, a large house for recovering patients. Then, having received their official papers, they were separated, with Jock returning home to Scotland and Ellis to the Battalion Headquarters in Wrexham.

One would have thought that Ellis, after all his tribulations, would now be excused from any further military service. But no, even though he was among two million British soldiers wounded in the Great War, like so many others he was returned to his battalion.

Having been in Wrexham for a week, I was given leave to return home for three weeks and then report back to Wrexham. I hadn't been home for three years... Going home made me very excited as everyone there knew about my facial injury. I cannot describe my feelings on that day as I walked home from the station, with everyone, I suppose, trying to catch a glimpse of me... Then my father appeared, but he failed to recognise me.

Three weeks later, Ellis is back in Wrexham among a hundred ex-patients with no mention of being discharged, although he and the others did have to visit a doctor daily. One morning, they were bemused to hear the order to go by lorry to collect their rifles. They refused to move. They also refused to follow orders the following day. A Sergeant Major arrived shouting loudly but he was ignored. Eventually, their rifles were taken to the train and the men forced to join them. This seems to have been a major incident, although it was played down by Ellis. The men's refusal amounted to mutiny and such a charge could have led to a court martial, and to the death penalty if found guilty. Ellis does not elaborate but the men obviously obeyed eventually.

Randalstown Camp in Ulster where Ellis served following his recovery

We were informed where we were going, and the place was Ireland. The Southern had been causing trouble. We reached Liverpool and on board ship I was a better sailor than I believed myself to be. I slept quietly throughout the voyage.

They docked in Dublin and travelled by train to Belfast and then on to a camp in County Antrim, twenty miles away. This was Randalstown. We are told very little of the political or military situation, despite the fact that 1918 was a stormy year in Ireland. Staunch Republicans and many of the more moderate Irish were fierce opponents of the Military Service Act (conscription). Until then, Ireland had been exempt. Ulster Unionists, on the other hand, were strongly in favour of the Act. Republicans called a general strike. Arthur Griffith won the East Cavan by-election for Sinn Féin. This led to the party sweeping to victory at the end of the year, winning 73 of the 103 constituencies. On the horizon loomed the 'Year of Terror' that would see the War of Independence and the arrival of the Black and Tans. But Ellis merely refers to the 'Southern' causing trouble.

Once more we have Ellis interested more in the quality of the Cavan soil and the farming customs of the inhabitants rather than in the political situation. The land was stony, he says, but the Irish were a frugal people making the best use of their situation. Living seemed to be hard and the cattle and horses seemed scrawny. This, he says, was a difficult and laborious life. The inhabitants and their animals looked poorly. He took the opportunity to visit neighbouring farms and chat with the farmers.

I observed their method of planting potatoes. They would place the potato on the grassy earth with some fifteen inches between the rows. Then they would cut turf on the opposite side; turn the turf over and then [begin] shovelling soil to form an even bed. Some rows were no more than six yards long, depending on the presence of a rock or large stone. But they would be careful in the whole preparation and would produce plenty of potatoes. The Irish were very enthusiastic potato eaters with every meal.

In the camp a Sergeant Lewis formed a singing group and Ellis joined in. Concerts were organised with solos, duets and performances by instrumental groups. One day the men were summoned to keep the peace during a street fracas following an incident, a killing on a Belfast street. But, says Ellis, they encountered few problems then or afterwards. Soon they were back where they began in North Wales, in Kinmel Camp near Rhyl.

There, Ellis did little more than kick his heels. His only duties were limited to attending the doctor's surgery and being present at the sick parade. The men could travel to town without having to pay. But the camp was hit by the flu. Many of the soldiers died. Two or three were buried daily, says Ellis. These funerals were military occasions with rifles fired over coffins. One day, Ellis witnessed four soldiers buried together. That flu led to the death of a quarter of a million in Britain. Indeed, more died from the effect of the flu within one year than were lost to the Black Death.

On one occasion, Ellis was strolling with some of his fellow soldiers out in the country. By chance, he met with Jac Henry, a younger brother who was with a crew of signallers. Ellis hadn't seen him for three years. Jac Henry, like Ellis, had been in

Ellis with his brother John Henry. They hadn't met for three years until they chanced upon each other

France, where he had injured his foot. Ellis then returned to Wrexham, where he received the long-awaited news of his discharge.

But his joy was short lived. There was no work awaiting him back home and he was forced to sign on the dole. This meant travelling to Blaenau Ffestiniog every Friday to collect his 25 shillings. Later, he found some part-time work delivering mail, and was afterwards employed as a haulier. This meant dragging tree trunks and ferrying goods from Maentwrog Station for Jones of Porthmadog, using horses that belonged to Hugh Davies of Hendre Mur. Ellis names some of his working colleagues as Thomas Jones, Dolgam; and Evan Rowland, Utica; both of whom

Ellis' release document having served three years and 10 months with the 38th

transported goods to and from Porthmadog Station.

Then he found himself again among the unemployed and on the dole, until fate took a hand; Ellis was out walking with Spot the dog when he chanced upon local squire Mr Vaughan of Nannau, Dolgellau, who was a shareholder with the Great Western Railway. He had known the squire since his time working at Llwyncrwn, when Mr Vaughan used to call to buy cattle that he would drive to London. Ellis asked the squire if he could help him find work.

Time passed slowly without any response. Eventually, a letter arrived inviting him to call at Trawsfynydd Station. There, he was given an English reading test and also tested for colour blindness by the station superintendent, a Mr Davies. Ellis passed successfully and was employed. He notes the date as 16 July 1918.

I remained with the railway until I retired. I began as a parcel porter at Bala Station. But this was only temporary. But I was there [with the railway company] *for 41 years until my retirement when 65 years old. During that time, I witnessed many changes. The work was only temporary until the lads returned from the war. During those nine months I was able*

to meet up again with old friends and colleagues from my
days working [as a farmhand] *at Llidiardau and*
Rhosygwalia, and also [made] *new friends.*

During this initial period, Ellis was involved with various
railway duties, including working as an engineer on the
Arenig to Tyddyn Bridge Halt length. It was located near
Frongoch, a village on the backroad between Trawsfynydd
and Bala.

From here on, Ellis, in his memoirs, limits himself to
discussing his love of singing and his role as a chorister
competing in meetings and eisteddfods, including the
Caernarfon National Eisteddfod of 1921, where his choir
won second prize. On that occasion, the Crown was won
by Cynan for his ode 'Mab y Bwthyn' ('Son of the Bothy'),
a poem that describes vividly the poet's experiences in the
Great War. Ellis goes on to describe himself singing with
various parties and choirs in competitions at Arenig,
Llidiardau, Talybont and Ty'n-y-bont. He refers to local
musicians and vocalists such as John Anthony Jones, Ed
Jones, and Watcyn Jones.

Wales is renowned for its *'Cythraul Canu',* literally
meaning 'The Demon of Song'. This refers to underhand
practices such as bribing adjudicators and favouritism, and
also much leg-pulling and provocation. We have Ellis
describing some of these practices, all with good humour.

Meanwhile, Ellis is moved to another length of railway,
to Cwm Prysor with Howel Jones of Bala as Ganger. In his
memoirs, he reminisces on competitions and choirs,
including the Prysor Male Voice Choir, conducted by J R
Jones, also known as 'Eos Prysor'. He relates how he joined
that choir and how he had been trained by his own father
to sing first tenor. He also refers to John Lloyd Edwards of
Blaenau, the choir's tutor.

Ellis recalls the party singing 'Martyrs of the Arena' in concert and reminisces about Parti Prysor and Parti Llanfor competing in eisteddfods. He recalls on one occasion, as members of his choir reached Bala Station, seeing the platform overflowing with well-wishers and relatives shouting their support. Bets were placed on the result, the sum of 25 shillings. Parti Prysor won. This, notes Ellis, was big money considering that the average weekly wage at the time was £2. Not all of his reminiscences are light-hearted, however.

I recall attending the New Year Eisteddfod at Dolgellau. Before the proceedings came to an end it started snowing heavily. We started for home but as we reached Ganllwyd the snow was deep and the wind had risen. We stopped, and the storm abated but the snow was too deep for the bus to continue. We began walking home. We reached home in the small hours of the morning. The effort proved too strenuous for one of us, Robin Vaughan as he was called. He died of the cold.

Suddenly, we reach the last entry.

In the year 1924 my father died of the old quarry disease aged 62. In the year 1925 I married Margaret Williams, Manchester House, daughter of Jane Williams and the late Lewis Williams the Shepherd.

That is the end of the written memoirs. But it is not the end of the story. Following Ellis' death in 1967, his widow, Margaret, applied for a widow's war pension as Ellis' death had been regarded as having been caused by coronary thrombosis. In other words, he had died of natural causes. Margaret maintained, quite correctly, that her husband had died from the after-effects of injuries suffered when he served as a soldier in the Great War. This had been disputed by the War Ministry.

In her letter of application, she noted that Ellis had served for three years and 59 days. She added that her husband had been discharged on 7 August 1918, on the grounds that he was unfit for war service. He had been awarded initially eighty percent of the full pension, or 32 shillings a week.

Margaret reasoned that the numerous operations her husband had suffered, including bone grafting and the reconstruction of his facial features, had led to the deterioration of his whole constitution. He had suffered with gangrene at Givenchy as a result of the effects of poison gas and had also suffered with frostbite. And, of course, he had suffered severe facial wounds at Mametz. The gangrene, she maintained, with backing from a doctor's report, had led to circulatory problems caused by blood clotting. Then, on 29 March 1966, one of his legs had needed to be amputated.

Margaret then confirms that this fact had been noted by her late husband in his recollections written in the form of a diary while he spent three months in hospital recovering from his amputation. As a result of the amputation, despite the fact that he had worked with the railway company, he had not been able to cope with heavy physical work. His experiences had led to continual headaches and shingles.

There is nothing to show whether Margaret's application was successful. But to have to apply in the first place was an outrage. As she noted at the end of her letter of application, her husband, Private Ellis Williams, No. 26129 of the Royal Welsh Fusiliers, had 'served his country bravely'.

Family Upheavals

Everyone has, at some time in life, encountered a watershed. At such a time, the decision taken may have seemed trivial, but another outcome might have led to a different future. Ellis experienced many such encounters.

Would he have been tempted to enlist if not for the time he spent, as a schoolboy, delivering letters at Bronaber Army Camp? There is also the matter of his refusal to continue as batman to the Adjutant, a move that would have saved him from the trenches. In addition to these, another missed opportunity exists, albeit through no fault of his own.

In 1907, an older brother, Evan Robert (otherwise known as Evan Bob) decided, when he was 21 years old, to emigrate to Patagonia. Four years later, two other brothers followed, Willie, aged 22; and Owen, aged seventeen. They were among the last contingent of Welsh immigrants to emigrate when they left on 2 November 1911. A ticket had also been bought for Ellis, who was fifteen, to sail with them on the *Oreta* from Liverpool.

Family historian Dwyryd Williams of Dolgellau has researched extensively into the family's Patagonian connections, and he believes that Ellis was prevented from leaving by William Williams, the father of the brothers, who felt bad enough at the prospect of losing three sons,

*Ellis' brothers in Patagonia: Robert with his wife Matilda
and her father, Hopkins Howells (front)
and William (Prysor) and Owen (standing).
The photograph dates around 1915.*

and so hid Ellis' ticket. It is worth noting that Dwyryd is the
great-grandson of another of Ellis' brothers, John Henry,
and is the grandnephew of Ellis.

According to Aunt Dilys of Trawsfynydd, Mrs Dilys
Lloyd Thomas, Uncle Ellis, who was the fourth son, had
also been booked for passage from Liverpool, but his
father snatched his ticket and burnt it. Uncle Ellis felt
reproachful about this for the rest of his life

Had Ellis been allowed to leave, he would have, of
course, avoided the war completely. According to the 1901
Census, William Williams was a 'Slate Quarry Rockman'. It
notes that his eldest son, Evan Robert, fifteen at the time,
was also a quarryman. According to Dwyryd, there were

William (Prysor) Williams (1889–1945) poet, author and musician. He won the Crown at the Welsh Patagonian Eisteddfod in 1921.

twelve children born to William and his wife Ellen.

It was said that there were so many children that some of them had to take turns to sleep in open drawers. But four children died young; Robert, the firstborn, died when he was only three, Kate at two months, Olwen four, and Mary, the last to be born, was only seven weeks old.

Why did Evan Bob venture to such a far-off country? Well, there were few opportunities for young people in the area to better their status within the local economy in those days. Most young men who did not work as farmhands had no alternative other than turning to quarrying at Blaenau Ffestiniog. It was hard and dangerous work. But being a farmhand was considered inferior and the wages were derisory. Quarrying carried more status. At the time, life in Patagonia, on the other hand, was slowly improving. The Welsh exiles had developed a system of canals to irrigate the land and agriculture was beginning to flourish. Indeed, there were more tractors and modern farm implements out there than there were in Wales.

Evan Bob would have written home extolling life out there, and in 1911 two of his brothers followed him. The young men, no doubt, could also sense what was about to happen in Europe. The clouds of war were gathering on the horizon and it is quite possible that this would have been a factor in their decision to leave.

Early in the 1800s, industry within the Welsh communities developed and this led to an exodus from the rural communities, in particular to the coalfields and the iron and steel works of South Wales. Many believed that Wales was now gradually being absorbed into England. A feeling of disillusionment and the opportunity for a new beginning attracted many Welshmen and women. The chief instigator for the Patagonian adventure was Michael D Jones, a Welsh Congregationalist minister from Bala. The three Williams brothers were among over a thousand who left between 1886 and 1911.

Two Chairs won by Prysor exhibited at the Gaiman Museum

Prysor's Crown exhibited in the Gaiman Museum

We learn that Evan Bob was an avid reader and a staunch Communist, and that the most prominent of the three was Willie. He had been a farmhand back home and had worked at Gors and further afield.

Having reached Patagonia, he settled in the Gaiman, close to his elder brother, where he prospered as a farmer. He was also a poet who adopted the bardic name Prysor. An eisteddfod Chair he won in 1920 can be seen at the Porth Madryn museum; a Chair won in 1921 and another Crown from 1918 are in the Gaiman museum. He became conductor of the Gaiman Children's Choir and was Deputy Archdruid of the colony's Gorsedd of Bards, as well as editor of the Welsh-language newspaper *Y Drafod* (*The Discussion*). He died suddenly while on a visit to Buenos Aires in 1945 and was buried there.

Owen ventured further across the prairie and settled at Cwm Hyfryd, near Trevelin and Esquel at the foot of the Andes, some three hundred miles away from his brothers. Thirty years were to pass before Evan Bob was able to meet up with Owen.

Dwyryd has gathered together a substantial family archive, including photographs and letters. The earliest letter among them was sent from Trawsfynydd on 9 February 1913, from William Williams to his son Owen. The family were then living at 13 Penygarreg Street.

The letter is rather nondescript, save for the father's anxiety regarding the lack of information on Willie's situation. He hadn't heard from him for some time. It is a mixture of local and world news, from referring to the death of a young quarryman to the sinking of the *Mauretania*. On the former, he notes:

A young man of 23 fell over the edge at the Oakeley [*Quarry*] last night and he died almost instantly.

Evan Robert and his wife Matilda and children Prysor, Islyn and Elis. One of them, Elis died in a swimming accident at the Plaza, Gaiman. Later three more children were born, Onen, Rhirid and Eri.

The tone of the comment, with its simple acceptance, suggests that such accidents were hardly unusual. There are references to local affairs, and to Wales' worsening economic situation, perhaps confirming the reason for his three sons' decision to emigrate. William Williams then comments on:

... some regular stirrings [*of people leaving*], no work available for anyone save for a few who are willing to work for farmers for a trifle. There are three leaving for the South tomorrow, Dei Penrallt, Will Llewelyn and Wil Jones.

Mary Vaughan, who later married Willie (middle)
with Willie and Owen (standing)

This reminds Dwyryd of the novel *William Jones* by T Rowland Hughes, published at a later time but dealing with the migration from the quarries of North Wales to the coalmines of South Wales.

We turn now to a letter sent by William Williams to Owen, dated 12 March 1916. It contains a significant passage:

I believe I have informed you that Ellis suffered a slight injury in France, having been hit in the head by a piece of shrapnel, though he didn't elaborate on that; the latest news from him is that he is quite well. On Friday night a message from him came through Dodo Jane, informing her that he had come through the treatment and was alive and once again feeling well and was very thankful for that; more so than ever as he had been an eye witness to one of his colleagues being mortally wounded, one who had grown up with him in this neighbourhood, Griffith Llywelyn, son of D Morris, my cousin. He did not elaborate but he said he had died peacefully and seemingly without any pain, telling the friend closest to him, 'Goodbye, I'm leaving you.' He was buried reverently on 5 March. His father wasn't present because of the distance… This is what will undoubtedly become of many of them; we know not when or what minute they will be harmed.

As the letter was dated around the middle of March, William Williams undoubtedly refers to the injury that tempted his son to rub soil into his wound to make it look worse. The second and the most serious injury did not occur until two months later. Regarding Ellis' description of Griffith Llywelyn Morris' death, Dwyryd believes that he was attempting to soften the blow by stating that his friend had died a peaceful and painless death. Dwyryd recalls his Aunt Dilys telling him that she remembered Ellis on more than one occasion describing Griffith Llywelyn's death in far more gruesome terms. We shall elaborate on this later.

It is worth noting that Dilys had lost her mother when she was only a few weeks old and was lovingly raised by Ellis and Margaret at their home in Maes Tegfryn. Her father had employed a number of housekeepers and eventually married one of them. Her stepmother, apparently, was antagonistic towards Dilys and her sister Nansi, and so Dilys was adopted by the pair. This led to her knowing Ellis better than most.

Returning to William Williams' letter, it illustrates vividly the intelligence of this simple quarryman in interpreting the war situation at the time. He tells Owen of his relief that the Germans' attempts to take Verdun had not yet succeeded, although scores, if not hundreds of thousands, had died. He opines that the destiny of the war depended on what happened there. Things looked favourable, with Russia continuing to scatter the Turks before them. The Turks, he states, were screaming for peace, complaining that the Germans had not supplied the necessary aid and equipment. He continues, stressing the danger of German U-boats to merchant shipping in the North Sea. He also comments on the danger from Zeppelins. He felt that the U-boats would have to choose very soon between exposing themselves and hiding in their boltholes until the end of the war. He continues:

> To tell you the truth, this war has now become a burden on countries and it would be a blessing if it all ended. And it is certain that there will be no peace but for a short period without subduing them [*the Germans*] completely.

He ends the letter by telling Owen that he had given Ellis' address to Mrs Hughes, Y Fron, the wife of Reverend Dafydd Hughes, minister of Moriah Chapel, the previous evening. A parcel from the Red Cross was expected soon containing underclothes, something the men would look forward to. He praises the good will shown by so many people from all over the land towards the soldiers.

In a letter sent to Owen in July 1920, we learn the

situation of one of William's sons in law. He worked alongside eight to ten others cutting peat near Tryweryn Lake for twelve shillings a day. In a letter written in October of the same year, we are provided with a picture of the social life in the area.

Singing is all go here now. I went with the choir to Ffestiniog; we were joint winners with Cor y Llan [*the Llan Choir*] there and also joint with the party of twelve singing two songs, and last night with the Tanygrisiau Choir where we won first prize – we are now preparing for battle at Dolgellau at the New Year Eisteddfod. I now recall that the Patagonia Eisteddfod will be held this month. I don't know whether you will be competing on the solo; I hope you will and that you will be successful. I understand that Willie is competing for the best poetry entry and I am confident that he also will reach the pinnacle.

William then refers to Ellis' situation. Ellis, he says, was now in a position that was common in the golden age of the railway. He also refers to the situation of the miners and the possibility of a strike.

Ellis is working on almost every Sunday now, as is the custom with platelayers occasionally, so you can see that he is earning good money but it is rather unpleasant to see him with his nose continually on the grindstone. The situation of the miners however looks grim. There was a call for a second ballot, and the great majority this time voted in favour should the Government not be prepared to meet with their demands. Both sides are stubborn and time is short. It is likely that the railwaymen will join them [*the miners*] and that the wheels of commerce will come to a halt pretty soon.

Ellis, in his memoirs of this period, replicates these sentiments. William then reminds us of the harshness of life back home as compared to life in Patagonia.

It was good to read in the letter you sent to Ellis that you will be receiving higher wages for your labour although having to move to find work. Gold is what everyone seeks; without gold, everyone will be left behind... But one should, at the same time remember that the gold from above purifies in the humane depths of the Divine Revelation. Doubtless, you and everyone else for that matter are earning big money. But is it easy to live there despite that with everything here is so massively expensive, train fares, rates, rents, clothes, bread, coal, boots and so forth all the way down to life's basic needs? What would you say to having to pay £3 or £3.5s for a pair of boots, almost £2 for half a hundredweight of coal? There is no hope of obtaining even the bare necessities.

In a letter to Owen, dated 17 October 1921, we learn that William has been suffering ill health. He goes on to state his position regarding work.

... I have by now recovered and ready for work but I haven't restarted yet. I have been promised work at the camp but it is likely that I will have to end up at the quarry once more, much as I would like to be out of it. We shall see.

It now becomes obvious that the exiled sons intend to

remain permanently in Patagonia. This grieves William deeply. He would love to see them back in Trawsfynydd. This is his reaction to the news that Owen has bought land:

> ... I hear that you are starting to claim areas of land out there; you are sinking your money in a most remote part of the creation. Should you decide to move sometime in the future it will not be easy to reclaim the land's value but maybe you are planning to remain there permanently.

A letter he wrote on 10 October, when 57 years old, notes that he is unwell.

> ... I have caught a bit of a cold, and that has reached my breast where it has been previously as bronchitis. But I have dragged myself to work up until now. I feel like staying at home for a week to try and rid myself of it. I was fine until I went to Pwllheli with the Manod singing party for some competition or other. We loitered on the way back with the weather being bitterly cold.

He then turns to Ellis' situation.

> Ellis has been working the Cwm Prysor length for a few weeks so he is now with us every night. He will be more content now. He did not enjoy the loneliness of the Arenig.

There are suggestions here and there of some dissent between father and exiled son. But this does not deter William from castigating the quarry owners in a letter to Owen dated 25 March.

The quarry company are trying to fathom how to

persuade us to work for the smallest sum of money, and to press us further. They have now announced that we will be limited to a five-day week, and you will realise, of course, which day of the week will be taken from us so that it will profit them. They will save themselves much money while their takings will suffer very little.

We now move on to 23 January 1925, and a letter from Winifred (Gwen), one of the daughters, and her husband, Dick, to the exiled brothers. It bears bad news regarding William's health. Then, on 18 May, we learn of William's death on 23 February. Dwyryd notes a poem written by local poet Glan Eiddon, which is seen on William's gravestone at Pencefn Cemetery.

Mab tawel ymhob tywydd – wele graith
    aml groes ar ei ysgwydd.
Dan ei gariad neu'i gerydd –
Ai'n nes i'w Dad nos a dydd.

(A quiet son in every weather – lo, the scar
    Of many a cross on his shoulder,
Beneath his love or censure –
Night or day, his Father is near.)

The letters from here on are tinged with some bitterness, with obvious conflict between Ellis and his sisters Mag and Nel. Soon after his father's death, Ellis got married. The sisters were forced to find work at the camp to help keep the wolf from the door. This annoyed Ellis. Meanwhile, Owen had offered to contribute towards the cost of his father's funeral. But in response, Ellis comments firstly regarding his sisters working at the camp:

People are talking about them everywhere regarding

the way they have turned their back on me to enable themselves to do as they please.

It is also obvious that Owen, in Patagonia, reacted positively to the request for a contribution towards the funeral costs and other expenses. But Ellis advises him not to be hasty, adding,

The reason I tell you this is that I believe that they would spend the money unwisely.

A letter from Nel to Owen, however, suggests that her brother had already contributed towards the funeral costs. But we learn that Ellis, a week following the funeral, has left home to live with his Uncle Tom. Despite the altercation between Ellis and his two sisters, it seems that he is still held in esteem by members of his choir. Ellis writes in a letter to Owen:

It was decided by the Male Voice Party to collect contributions around the area towards my father [*his funeral costs*] without consulting me. I thought about it and remembered how much against the grain it had been to my father when they had collected previously when my mother was bad. I also felt like that this time but felt too humble to refuse unless things got too hopeless for me... so having considered it, I opposed collecting round the neighbourhood for him. So I unforgivably sinned. The singing party however collected among themselves to honour the memory of his membership. As I had opposed the collection I was not told but I heard from others what the total collected came to. It was, I believe, £3.

It seems, therefore, that Ellis had too much self-respect to accept charity. It also becomes obvious that the same obstinacy was shared by his sister Nel. In a letter to Owen, she writes that she is now working as a housekeeper for a local resident and is determined to maintain the family home. She is, however, prepared to accept contributions from her brothers in exile.

Dwyryd also has a letter sent by Ellis to Owen, written in early October 1919. In it, he refers to the harvest at Trawsfynydd.

We haven't had any kind of harvest; it has been so cold and wet. There is so much hay lying around and no hope now of harvesting it. The corn hasn't been cut either – very few have managed to harvest anything and what is left is rotting and no sign of good weather to dry it. Today is the first day of October. We are also suffering with heavy showers of hail that destroys all the crops.

He goes on to complain about the religious decline locally. Dwyryd reminds us that the period between the two 'world wars' has been regarded as a kind of golden age for religion. But obviously, he adds, this wasn't so. Ellis continues:

Trawsfynydd has become a distinctly chapel-free place. The young think nothing of chapel. I believe this will become a very strange place before very long. Parents no longer even contemplate sending their children to chapel. But should there be living pictures or a dance or something similar held, then the hall will be full on such occasions. You might see some twenty at the Sunday morning prayer meeting from among three hundred members, around ten to fifteen at the Wednesday night meeting... neither are they interested in singing. The floor was only half filled last night for the Methodist singing festival. I don't know how many will be present tonight.

The change in the nature of the society is to be seen in his reference to a motoring accident. As Dwyryd notes, cars were something of a novelty at Trawsfynydd in 1929.

Will Bach, Nantbudur, was returning home from somewhere or other recently when near Berthu he was hit by a motor car, injuring his head. He was quite strange for a fortnight or three weeks. He was rather confused and uttered some strange things at the time. But he is recovering. You can imagine the things William was saying as he is so funny anyway.

In his letter to Owen, we have an unexpected comment by Ellis. While accepting the fact that Owen has recently married, he comments on having children and of the problems of rearing them.

I do not know what I should tell your wife – maybe it would be better if I should write to her after I hear from her first. It isn't easy writing to someone you don't know but may I hope that you will both be happy and that you will long remain childless so that you may be free to enjoy yourselves for a while before you start raising children. Otherwise you will have to take them with you everywhere or stay at home caring for them. Thus I am still without children. That's the way of things, we are reluctant to see them arrive and we don't want to lose them after they arrive. The longer the better, I say.

This is an unusual comment as he loved children, as will be elaborated on later. But it is easy to understand his sentiments regarding having children only to lose them. Four of his siblings had died young, a brother and three sisters. He had also witnessed the terrible deaths of comrades on the battlefield, no doubt most of them leaving grieving parents behind.

It is worth noting here that it was Owen and his wife Blodwen who raised Elvira Austin, who came to live in Wales in the 1960s to study at Harlech College. She became well known as hostess on the television series *Siôn a Siân*, the Welsh version of *Mr and Mrs*, for some eighteen months. Elvira's mother had died after being shot. Some believe that a gun went off accidentally while being handled in the house. Others talk of her washing clothes in a nearby brook when she was hit by a hunter's stray bullet. Elvira was only two days old at the time and was adopted by Owen and Blodwen. She now lives at Baglan near Port Talbot.

Obviously Dwyryd Williams has in his possession an important archive, both written and photographic, of his family history. It is indeed of national importance in the context of the history of Wales' Patagonian connections. Here, I have merely referred to those letters which pertain to Ellis' involvement in the war and his social situation in the Trawsfynydd area. And, of course, the consequences of those events that contrived to prevent him from emigrating to Patagonia.

My Uncle Ellis

To former soldiers who have experienced the heat of battle, it is always their families who are among the last to hear of their experiences. War heroes seldom talk of their actions. This was particularly true of Ellis, or 'Unc', as he was called by his two nieces, Nansi and Dilys Lloyd, who fondly remember him. Nansi has said:

> You would have thought that he would have wanted to relive the experience. But he never mentioned it. I never once heard him complain.

Dilys, having been brought up by Ellis and Margaret, knew him better than most. The only war incident she heard him mention was the death of a close friend.

> I well remember him talking of the death of a friend who was blown up. He described how Bobi Morus of Traws' brains landed in his hands in the trench. He would mention that quite often. But otherwise, nothing.

This event was referred to in the previous chapter by Dwyryd Williams, the description of the death much sanitised in Ellis' letter home. Having witnessed such gory scenes, it is easy to appreciate why he was so reticent in

Uncle Ellis, best man at John Henry's wedding with bride
Dorothy (Dol) Roberts and her sister Elizabeth c. 1921.
John Henry and Dol were Dwyryd Williams' grandparents.

recalling his experiences. Whether he expected anyone to read his memoirs is a question that can't be answered. Certainly, had this author not read his memoirs in that little blue exercise book, I would not have known a quarter of his story.

I can't recall during my childhood ever hearing Uncle Ellis mention the war or his experiences. I don't believe he shared his war experience with anyone. He was an avid reader, his home full of books. And among those books at Maes Tegfryn was the copy book, a form of diary recorded in retrospect rather than contemporaneously. I inherited all his books but I did not clear the house until his widow, Aunt Maggie, died some years later. I remember turning to the opening page of the copy book and glancing over it. It seemed to be just an ordinary diary. It opened with recollections of his life as a youngster in Trawsfynydd, followed by those of his life as a farmhand here and there. It did not promise to be all that interesting. I put it to one side and only returned to it much later. I read it through and realised I hadn't really known Uncle Ellis at all despite the fact that I had been close to him. No, I hadn't known him at all.

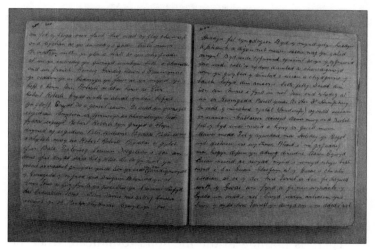

Two pages from Ellis' diary recorded painstakingly in an exercise book

As I read it in detail that very first time I had to put it down occasionally because of the emotion I felt. I was in tears. I spent nights poring over it, devouring it. It took time as I could only manage three or four pages per session.

Ellis died when I was around eleven years old. My memories of him go back to my childhood when I was around five or six. I would sit on his knee and I still remember fondling his face and thinking his face wasn't like other people's faces. I would touch his nose. Yes, it was his nose that was different. Indeed, like the Queen years previously in that hospital at Boulogne, I would tweak his

With Uncle Ellis during a visit to Rhyl

nose. And he would just sit there quiet and unmoving without even pushing my hand away. I was none the wiser. At that age I had no idea why he was different. And I was too young to think of asking him why.

There is nothing in the memoirs to indicate when he recorded them. But Margaret's letter of application for the full widow's pension mentions her late husband's reference to his injuries having been noted in writing during his period of recuperation after amputation. There is little doubt that she was referring to a relevant section of the copy book. The letter refers to Ellis suffering from the long-term effects of poison gas and Margaret in her letter attributes the amputation to gangrene caused by gas in 1916. Typically, in his memoirs, Ellis understates the danger of poison gas, mentioning it only once.

He spent weeks in hospital following the amputation. I remember visiting him there. He must have written his memoirs during this period. But I still ask myself why he did so. I have a feeling it was his way of finding closure. It must have been a form of catharsis.

As both of my grandfathers had long died, I regarded Uncle Ellis as the grandfather I didn't have. He was the one who taught me everything. He would take me fishing along the banks of the Prysor using a worm or a fly as bait. He taught me the names of the various pools, Llyn Trobwll (Whirlpool Lake) and Llyn Ceffyl Du (Black Horse Lake). He loved nature. He would take me walking around the countryside. One day we both disappeared for a whole day, causing my mother to worry as night fell.

When he wasn't wandering around he would spend his time in the little black shed in the garden. I would sit with him for hours. He owned a set of carpenter's tools including a whole collection of chisels. He loved carving. I remember a plaque he made with the words of a proverb carved into it, *'Cadw dy afraid erbyn dy raid'* (Keep your inessentials until you need them). In the shed he found peace and tranquillity. He would often play draughts. There would always be a set on the kitchen table. I would

With Uncle Ellis and Aunty Margaret on the beach at Rhyl

With sister Caroline and Uncle Ellis at Rhyl

spend hours playing against him.

Local historian Keith O'Brien, who is curator of the Trawsfynydd Heritage Centre, has a theory as to why Ellis decided to write his memoirs rather than discuss them, and on his reluctance to reveal his exploits in the trenches.

It is possible that by jotting words on paper he could express himself easier than he would have made through conversing face to face with others. That, of course, is a pity in a way. But it is fortunate that he did record them on paper or otherwise we would have been none the wiser of his experiences.

Keith also offers an answer to the question of why Ellis decided to volunteer his services.

Nationalistic propaganda, of course, lauded voluntary enlistment as men who joined would become heroes by defending their country. It was, of course, naivety and innocence. And certainly, any opportunity for a young lad to wear a uniform and carry a gun and return a hero was tempting. Wow! They believed they would live forever! The possibility of being killed never entered their minds. Adventure and patriotism, those were the twin attractions although they had no idea what awaited them. They would be taught to march and to fire weapons. And how they would enjoy this new life far away from the banality of home.

Uncle Ellis and Aunty Margaret far from the hell of Mametz

Like so many alive who knew him, Keith has only childhood memories of Ellis.

> We tended, as children, to view him as someone who was a little different because of the scars on his face. We would view him from afar, trying to imagine what had happened to him. Had he been born like that? Had he been involved in an accident? And not being able to imagine what had really happened to him.

Keith O'Brien tried to imagine the totally different way of living experienced by Ellis as a soldier.

It was a totally different world to the one he had

Ellis and Margaret relaxing following Ellis release from serving with the 38th

experienced in the Welsh countryside where he would watch over a few sheep and milk a cow or two. Then he found himself struggling through smoke and water. Shooting. Firing. And of course the most frightening aspect would have been the big guns, the artillery. Not only the fact that they were in essence engines for grinding and mincing, they were the most destructive machines in existence. Then there were the psychological effects. The shell whistling overhead and no-one knowing where it would land. One might have just landed on a comrade, his head blown away but his legs still running. Terrible experiences, the most hideous ever known.

Ellis' disillusionment was deepened when he suffered those early injuries that necessitated treatment. Ellis, as he confessed in his jottings, attempted to make the wounds appear worse than they really were. He was beginning to see beyond the deception and the jingoism.

There are passages in the memoirs where one can sense he felt that enough was enough, physically and mentally. This culminated with the event described above when he rubbed earth in his wounds in the hope that it would lead to being sent home to Britain. But he was sent back to the trenches and injured again, far more seriously this time.

That's what it was all about; being plied with tots of rum before being ordered over the top. That was their life; and very often their death. They witnessed comrades dying all around them. And that element of luck should the bullet that was meant to kill you missed, often hitting someone else.

The Great War, says Keith, was regarded as a modern war, with every soldier doing what he thought he should do:

> That's what his country expected of him. That's what his country had asked him to do. And he would be greatly rewarded for defending the free world that they were so privileged to be a part of. And they, not understanding or knowing any better.

You would expect someone who experienced so much atrocity to have become embittered. But no, Uncle Ellis was a gentle character and upon looking back and reading his memoirs it is difficult to believe how meek he was despite all his suffering. He was always kind-mannered and everyone liked him. He did have a temper; he admitted that. He was also mischievous. Aunt Maggie on the other hand was rather straitlaced, a devout chapel-goer. So Ellis would sometimes sneak into my mother's house where he would down a bottle of Guinness. Otherwise, because of his love for woodworking, he would spend a lot of his time in the shed. It was there, I believe, that he found the peace and quiet he craved, where he could contemplate the past.

You would also expect him, after all he had suffered on the battlefield, to hate Germans. But the opposite was true. Dilys Lloyd remembers him telling her that when he was almost unconscious following his injury, he heard some Welsh soldiers passing him. One of them said, 'Leave him

Ellis and Margaret with an unknown couple

to die.' Then some Germans came along and he heard them discussing him: 'He's still alive; we'll save him.' He never elaborated on whether they were instrumental in calling for help, but every time he saw Germans on television he would salute them.

I believe that luck played a huge part in his survival. He lay for hours in the mud. He could vaguely hear soldiers passing and words such as, 'He's dead; he'll never make it.' Yet he did not return a pacifist. He merely accepted what had happened. That's how things were. He was a soldier. Such things happened to soldiers. That's how he felt despite concealing the memory of all the atrocities he experienced.

I often wonder, when he returned for the first time following his long treatment, what went through his mind? Old friends must have stared at him with his new face. What would have been his reaction? What would have been their reaction? Keith O'Brien has often thought about this:

What did people see when they looked at this man who was so different in his appearance to the man he once

Aunty Margaret and Aunty Nell, the Rev and Mrs D.T. Morris and Uncle Tom and Uncle Ellis. The Rev Morris was the local minister.

was? It is likely that he had changed psychologically as well. Visually he was obviously not the same person who had left the area three years previously. And the fact that he was the object of curiosity must have been obvious to Ellis as well. But like all returning soldiers, he must have been happy to be home from the hell that was war and among kith and kin once more.

Outwardly, at least, he readjusted to village life, although I do ponder on how he managed to do that following such traumatic experiences. He took up employment some two or three years following his return. Indeed, he continued working on the railway until he was comparatively old. He was both sociable and popular. His closest friend was Idris Wyn, who kept a shop across the street. Even after his amputation he would go and watch football matches with Idris. He loved football and had

Prysor Rangers 1920–21 with Ellis on the right in the middle row.
Sitting in front of the minister is John Henry.

played for the local team even after his long treatment. There is a team photograph that includes Ellis. Considering the extent of his injuries, he was a brave man to even contemplate playing. But he was fit and strong. Then, following his amputation, he regularly travelled to support such teams as Porthmadog, Caernarfon and Cricieth. He would hardly miss a Saturday match, with Idris Wyn driving him to some venue or other. He once presented me with an old pair of football boots. They were big with leather studs. It was somehow appropriate that it was at a football match he suffered what turned out to be his last illness.

Following the amputation, he was seen regularly roaming around the village on his crutches. He refused the offer of a prosthetic leg. He would fold his spare trouser leg up to his thigh and used a safety pin to keep it in place.

When he worked on the railway, he would bring home sleepers that had been replaced. He would saw them into short lengths and chop them up as firewood and I would sell them in bundles around the village. He worked the busiest length between Bala and Trawsfynydd. During the winter months, snow would often close the line. He loved taking me along to show me the steam engine.

As someone who was raised towards the end of the 1950s and the beginning of the 1960s, Keith O'Brien never witnessed either of the 'world wars'. But he did witness their effect on ex-servicemen, both physically and psychologically.

Ellis and Margaret in the garden of their home at Maes Tegfryn c. early 60s

I saw simple, ordinary men who had been through various campaigns when they were youngsters, many who could not even contemplate returning home to their families. It is imperative that we do not forget such men.

There were awkward situations occasionally. Dilys remembers one in particular:

I remember being with him during a visit to Llandudno. He drove an old Austin 7 and just before we started for home he had to go to the toilet. As he went, he came face to face with a mother and her small son. The boy, seeing Ellis, turned to his mother and said, 'Look, mam, he's got a face like a monkey!' That's the only occasion for me to see him totally broken. He was really hurt that day.

The memoirs mean a lot to me. They chronicle the experiences of a common man. Uncle Ellis would never have been famous. He had no wish to be famous. But to me he was a hero. Even without knowing of his wartime exploits he would still have been a hero to me.

I don't know whether he would have been happy today if he knew his memoirs had been shared with the reading public. But it was important to me that his story should be told, as it represents thousands of other unknown heroes. Most of those who returned bearing wounds did not relate their story. But now, even with Uncle Ellis long dead, he still speaks. And he speaks for them all, those who made it home and those who still lie in and around Mametz Wood.

Private Ellis Williams' military medals and badges

Afterword

An accusation of cowardice is the worst slur that any soldier can suffer. But that is the slur that the men of the 38th had to carry for years. Today, thanks to research and foraging by historians, that stain has been gradually erased. It took time. Indeed, it took over seventy years before the men of the 38th were adequately honoured in 1987 with a fitting memorial on the site where so many were massacred and maimed. The venture, which meant raising £20,000 through voluntary contributions, was initiated by the South Wales branch of the Western Front Association. It was partly supported by the Welsh Assembly.

The sculptor commissioned to design and execute the work was David Petersen of St Clears. Central to it is the Welsh Dragon of Wales standing on a slate plinth. Rather than glorifying war, Peterson decided his work would reflect the bravery of the men who fought there. It also symbolises the futility of war. The Dragon turns its head towards the woods, holding in one of its paws a length of torn barbed wire. This denotes the ending of the war. The Dragon is cast in steel although originally intended to be cast in bronze. Financial constraints meant going for the cheaper option. Yet, isn't steel most appropriate? Did not the men of the 38th exhibit steel of the finest, the shiniest and the hardest?

The plinth on which the steel Dragon stands was quarried in the Forest of Dean. It was intended to be Welsh slate. But again, financial constraints put an end to that idea. On it are carved the insignias of three regiments. These are the South Wales Borderers, the Royal Welsh Regiment and the Royal Welsh Fusiliers. Accompanying the insignias are the words:

Parchwn eu hymdrechion, parhaed ein hatgofion
(We honour their endeavour, may our memories endure)

The author of those words, although her name is not recorded, is Avril Jones, formerly of Derwen Gam, Ceredigion, and now living in Cardiff. She was present at the unveiling ceremony when a number of survivors gathered to present wreathes and to stand to attention while two buglers sounded 'the Last Post'. Present was the band of the 1st Battalion of the Royal Welsh Regiment, as was the regimental mascot Taffy the goat. The singing was led by the Cilgeti Male Voice Choir. Not present were those that fell, although many of them were close by, resting in graveyards and others still lying in the nearby woods. Others, like Ellis Williams, had died later of the effects brought on by injuries suffered during that terrible July a century ago.

Today, Mametz Wood is quiet save for the twittering of little birds punctuated by the shrieks of hawks. Predominantly, however, there is little to be heard but for the sighing of the wind blowing among the branches. Such were the comforting sounds heard by Ellis Williams drifting from the Glasfryn woods long ago. Mametz Wood is a graveyard now. There is peace also in Pencefn Cemetery back in Trawsfynydd where rests a man who went into a hell and came back to write his story. His memoirs were meant for him, and for him alone. But it is a story that deserves retelling.

You have now, like me, had the honour of reading it.

Addendum

The following is a translation of extracts from a Welsh poem, 'Brwydr y Coed' ('The Battle of the Woods'). It was written under the pseudonym '*Un o'r Ffosydd*' (Someone from the Trenches) and appeared in *Y Dinesydd Cymreig*, 25 September 1918. The translator is unnamed.

The complete Welsh version appeared in *Y Cymro* on 7 August 1918. The author probably belonged to the 16th Royal Welsh Fusiliers. The poem quotes Lieutenant Colonel Carden's now famous 'On, Welshmen, on!' speech, and is based on the story of the men going into the attack while singing hymns, as quoted by both 14th and Royal Welsh Fusiliers battalion diaries.

THE BATTLE OF THE WOODS

The General's orders arrived in the trenches –
'Stand to with your bayonets attached.
We attack the Germans; dug deep in the woodlands;
From the trees he'll be swiftly dispatched.'

The night turned to first-light, then dawn was upon us;
The most wondrous morning of all –
As we stood in close order awaiting the order
'Attack! Take those trees. That's your goal!'

The CO said 'Welshmen! Be proud of your homeland,
The greatest of efforts' expected today.
Pray to the God of your parents and loved-ones,
For the woods to be taken, and the Germans we slay!'

The lads started singing, a hymn full of longing,
The mournful close harmonies cutting the breeze
Sweetly the melodies soared from the trenches –
As the seconds ticked down. Then we went for those trees!

Through horrors of fighting, the deaths and the screaming;
The Welsh were victorious; we'd done all we could.
Our ranks were depleted, friends unaccounted
As we buried their remnants at the edge of the wood.